DATE DUE

~~DE 1'97~~			
~~NO 3'98~~			
~~NO 14'98~~			
MY 3'99 RENEW			
~~MY 27'99~~			
~~AP 27'07~~			

DEMCO 38-296

Prison Sexual Violence

Prison Sexual Violence

Daniel Lockwood

Elsevier · New York
New York · Oxford

Elsevier North Holland
52 Vanderbilt Avenue, New York, New York 10017

Distributors outside the United States and Canada:

Thomond Books
(A Division of Elsevier/North-Holland Scientific Publishers, Ltd.)
P.O. Box 85
Limerick, Ireland

Library of Congress Cataloging in Publication Data

Lockwood, Daniel, 1944–
    Prison sexual violence.
    Originally presented as the author's thesis, State University of New York
    at Albany.

    Bibliography: p.
    Includes index.
    1. Prisoners—New York (State)—Sexual behavior. 2. Prison violence—
    New York (State) I. Title.
HV8836.L63   1979   365'.64   79-19376
ISBN 0-444-99067-4

Desk Editor   Michael Gnat
Design   Edmée Froment
Mechanicals   José Garcia
Production Manager   Joanne Jay
Compositor   Publishers Phototype Inc.
Printer   Haddon Craftsmen

Manufactured in the United States of America

For Evie

Contents

Acknowledgments

I wish to acknowledge my great debt to the hundreds of New York State prisoners who, patiently and enthusiastically, shared with me their experiences and ideas. The cooperation of the New York State Department of Correctional Services made this collaboration possible; I especially thank Earl Mayo, Fran Mills, and John Parker for assisting me in contacting interviewees. Financial support for the research came entirely from the Law Enforcement Assistance Administration: I gathered the data under the aegis of an LEAA research grant ("Interventions for Inmate Survival") and a Graduate Research Fellowship from LEAA supported me for the year it took to analyze the data.

I thank the faculty of the School of Criminal Justice of the State University of New York at Albany for nurturing my growth in this field. Hal Pepinsky, Graeme Newman, and Travis Hirschi were especially helpful. I am grateful to Robert Hardt and William Brown, members of my dissertation committee, for their diligent assistance. Michael Gottfredson and Commissioner Stephen Chinlund suggested meaningful changes. I owe much to my colleagues on the "Interventions" grant—particularly James Fox, John Gibbs, and Bob Johnson—for sharing with me their expertise and skill. Hans Toch, chairman of my dissertation committee and director of the "Interventions" grant, guided and encouraged me from the time I presented a paper on prison rape to his class on violence to the time I defended the dissertation four years later.

Linda Beecher and Kathy Schmidt transcribed the interviews. Phyllis R. Hladik, skillful and dedicated, typed excerpts and preliminary drafts. I am indebted to David Wicks for his fine job of coding the interviews and making the incident diagrams. Eileen D'Agostino Joann Colucci, and Jean Moschetto of the College of Technology typed the final copy. I express special thanks to Lee Bowker and Donna Hall for their valuable comments on the manuscript. A final word of thanks goes to William Gum at Elsevier, who prompted me to rewrite the dissertation and then applied his editorial genius to this book. I alone, however, am responsible for errors.

Foreword

As social scientists, we have been accused—
and often justly—of studying trivia, of map-
ping the exposed tips of icebergs, and ignoring
the overwhelming meaning and impact of
their submerged substance. *Prison Sexual Violence* is an exploration of the submerged. It
joins in spirit, if not in form, the classics of
world literature that have given us a sense of
the bowels of prison, of the cutting edge of the punishing experience we unwittingly inflict on men who have transgressed.

This book makes a landmark contribution, not just because it viv-
idly portrays a hidden world, but because it does this with passion-
ate dispassionateness and disciplined love. Daniel Lockwood, in this
rare book, provides a unique blend of deep concern for suffering
with respect for appropriate level of documentation and evidence.
His work is all the more remarkable because it is done against the
shrill chorus of ideology and dogmatism that undergirds the social
movement for radical prison reform. Ironically, it is *because* this book
is good social science that it serves the cause of the inmate most effectively, contrasting sharply with the aridity of sanctimonious ser-
mons and heated pronouncements that leave us jaded.

Prisons stand in desperate need of reform. This is not primarily
because prisons are evil, but because they contain evil, and because
such evil embodies the problems prisons ostensibly redress. For if
we say that men are imprisoned for inflicting suffering on others, it

is intolerable that the level of suffering within prison parallels or exceeds suffering that criminals inflict on victims. This is all the more true because we gravitate, within prison, to solutions that are clones of the evil, in the sense that we create prisons-within-prison to contain intramural aggressors or victims.

I do not suggest that we are collectively callous or callously malevolent. I know prison wardens and guards who resonate to inmate suffering and deplore victimization as much or more than do academics or critics of prison. Their problem lies in the limits of our knowledge, and in the restriction of remedial options available to them. It is for this reason that *Prison Sexual Violence* becomes mandatory reading for correctional officials at all levels.

The book, though, is more than a prison book, and it delivers more than is suggested by its title. This is true because the persons described in this book—as human beings—have continuity that transcends prison walls. The roles such persons play—as victims and transgressors, bullies and scapegoats, exploited and exploiters—are universal roles, and the sorts of sad encounters described in *Prison Sexual Violence* recur, with disquieting chronicity, around us. It is not simply that prison victimizers exploit others—women, for instance—in their homes and in the streets. It is also that the essence of scapegoating or bullying, deriving self-esteem at someone else's expense, should strike us as a perennial fact of life. For it is here that we encounter the egocentric norms and sadistic dynamics to which no human institution or individual seems immune.

In scenes described in Lockwood's book, we see men feeding on men in ways that are not only truly primeval but reflective of advanced rules of our societal games. The repulsive, disgusting, offensive depravity we must face and reject in Lockwood's account links us disquietingly to ourselves. It bids us attend to our consciences, our conceits, our yardsticks of worth, and (above all) our uses of power. For it is in man's ascendency over man and in his painful submission, that we find the key dilemmas posed by *Prison Sexual Violence.*

Hans Toch

Prison Sexual Violence

Researching Prison Sexual Violence

 Sexual aggression, to an extent, characterizes a certain percentage of all erotic encounters in our culture, regardless of social position (Kanin, 1965). Sexual aggression in male prisons is one part of this more general condition. As Sykes (1971) notes about the prison aggressor, "His perversion is a form of rape and his victim happens to be a man rather than a woman, due to force of circumstances" (p. 97).

Prison sexual aggression is thus unique in that the targets are men. The masculine response to sexual threat portrayed in this book brings out significant themes for the general study of male behavior. For example, the meaning of homosexuality colors and shapes the phenomena we study here. Some of the stress following victimization can be related to some men's horror of appearing homosexual. The intensity connected to the average male's desire for a masculine image is an issue for both aggressors and victims.

The study of prison sexual aggression is a study of violence. To the extent that either aggressors or targets may become violent, the outcome is related to other types of violence caused by interactions rather than original intentions. Force escalating beyond the intent of participants, problems of communication, and responses resulting from fear or slighted pride—these are features of violent interactions ranging from family quarrels to international warfare. Prison sexual violence is a case study of escalating violence.

In addition to the concerns of sexuality and violence, this book contributes to the general issue of race and crime. In prison, most aggressors are black; most targets are white. Prison sexual aggression, thus, is a case study of interracial crime. White racism follows from or is reenforced by the predatory actions of blacks. Fear of attack becomes fear of blacks. Why are whites targets? Why are blacks aggressors? What are the effects of the racial pattern of victimization? This book deals with such questions.

Sexual aggression, for some men, is a main contributor to the impact of the prison experience. To inmates in a penitentiary, the formal structure of a prison, its planned work, recreation, and rehabilitation programs, may be a thin veneer. The "real" world of truly significant events comes from the informal social environment created by the convict community. Sexual aggression, a component of this social environment, exemplifies the hold informal processes have and will continue to have on life in total institutions. This book thus reports on a research project that delved deeply into one traditional feature of prison life in America—sexual violence.

RESEARCH SETTING

In 1974 and 1975, using transcribed interviews and background data from prison files, I examined 107 "targets" of sexual aggressors and 45 inmate "aggressors" living in New York State male prisons. Targets were compared statistically to "nontargets," and aggressors were systematically compared to a control group. Interview material traced the impact of sexual victimization on targets and presented the aggressors' viewpoint. Data relating to staff handling of the problem were also accumulated. While some targets and all aggressors were located by any means possible, a random survey was also conducted. This survey found that 28 percent of prisoners interviewed had been targets of sexual aggressors at least once in institutional custody. Only one inmate in the random sample had been sexually assaulted, suggesting that prevalence of prison rape among New York State prisoners is low relative to other categories of harm accompanying sexual incidents. This harm included inmates being abused physically, abused by threatening or insulting language, and subjected to propositions that they perceived as threatening.

I gathered this material while working for a federally funded research project called "Interventions for Inmate Survival." As a staff member on this grant, I had free access to New York State prison records, prison staff, and prisoners. Psychologist Hans Toch directed the project. It followed methods he had successfully deployed previously in studies of crisis and conflict among prison inmates and police (Toch, 1969, 1975, 1977). In this methodology, clinical and social psychology are applied to problems experienced by clients of the system. Researchers examine reconstructed critical incidents with extreme care. Open-ended interviews, tape recorded and transcribed, catalog subjects' concerns in their own language. The mass of information is then content analyzed (Holsti, 1969). This book, therefore, is best seen as the product of a "school," whose mentor is Hans Toch. It joins a list of meticulously constructed works, based on transcribed interviews with large numbers of prisoners, that have put on the public record the intensely personal experiences of incarcerated men and women in New York State (Toch, 1975; Johnson, 1976; Fox, 1976; Gibbs, 1978). Since the prisoners interviewed were, for the most part, unable to have their experiences published, these works speak for them. Without such research, their experiences would have been lost, without any benefit. Hopefully, the record of these prisoner's experiences, recorded in the works of Toch and his students, will have an impact on correctional policy in this country.

The "Interventions" project, funded by the federal government, was an inquiry into the psychological needs of prisoners and the psychological attributes of prison settings. Looking at ways to match man to environment, the project sought to improve prisoners' chances of psychological survival in confinement (Toch, 1977). The study of sexual aggression fit neatly into this grant because some prisoners have a predominant need for safety. To the extent that sexual aggression makes prison a place of fear, targets of such aggression are plausible clients for "intervention for inmate survival." Thus, as a research associate on this project, I was supported by the grant to study sexual aggression in New York's prisons. My work on the grant resulted in the completion of my doctoral dissertation, "Sexual aggression among male prisoners." To reach a more general audience, and to achieve greater brevity and readability, I have modified the original dissertation considerably in writing this book. Thus, the reader concerned with such matters as tables and statistical analysis is advised to consult my Ph.D. dissertation (Lockwood, 1977b) for the complete empirical framework undergirding my conclusions.

The staff of the New York State Department of Correctional Services willingly cooperated with the "Interventions" project. Generally, staff viewed the project as an enterprise offering solutions to important problems. Consequently, I experienced complete cooperation. Staff gave me access to all records, provided private interviewing rooms, and "called out" any prisoners and employees I wished to interview. At a seminar held for Department staff in Albany, I had the opportunity to report some of my research findings to prison officials.

When the grant for "Interventions" ended, a Graduate Research Fellowship from the Law Enforcement Assistance Administration supported me for the year it took to analyze my data and write the dissertation. Without this generous contribution, the information described here would still be locked in thousands of pages of interviews and data sheets. The cooperation I received and the considerable resources diverted to my independent inquiry should dispel the notion that New York State and federal officials are totally unconcerned about prison sexual aggression. As we will see in the following chapters, prison sexual aggression is a problem in New York State prisons, not so much because of lack of official concern, but because of the social and psychological dynamics involved. These dynamics are the subject of this book. Before presenting research findings from New York State, I will review what is known about the general prevalence of prison sexual violence.

PREVALENCE: A Review of the Literature

Throughout the United States, for a considerable period of time, sexual aggression has been reported as being a major problem in male prisons. Journalists have commented on it on numerous occasions. For example, in 1971, Linda Carlton reported in *The New York Times* the "Terrifying homosexual world of the jail system." Wayne King (1975), reporting on overcrowding in Florida's prison system, noted officials' helplessness in controlling sexual aggression in the Glades State Prison. Within a two month period, in my local area, the Albany *Times Union* (1975a,b) ran such stories as "Escapee tells of prison attacks" and "6 indicted in sodomy at Dutchess County Jail."

Lawmakers have been aware of the problem. In 1975, for example, employees of the New York State Commission of Corrections, testifing before a hearing held by the Senate Standing Committee on Crime and Correction, described how two prisoners were sexually assaulted over a five-day period in the Schenectady County Jail. A report of the Federal House Judiciary subcommittee, headed by Representative Robert W. Kastenmeir, mentioned sexual abuse among the problems it found by visiting prisons and hearing testimony (*New York Times*, 1974a). The most significant government in-

4

vestigation of male sexual aggression in confinement so far is the report on the Philadelphia prison system carried out by the District Attorney's office and the Police Department (Davis, 1968a). This investigation received widespread media coverage at the time .

Reports such as those mentioned here have little to say about sexual violence in women's prisons. Prisons for women, evidence suggests, experience far less sexual aggression than prison for men (Brownmiller, 1975; Giallombardo, 1966). One reason is that males in our culture are more violent than females (Nettler, 1977). Also, women in prison often form themselves into "families." One prisoner will take the role of "husband," another of "wife," another as "child," and so on, until an extended protective and supportive and closely knit group is created. Absent in male prisons, the "family" can protect female prisoners without necessarily exploiting them. A further reason why female prisons have less sexual violence than male prisons is that women, who are more accustomed to being propositioned than men, react less strongly to nonviolent sexual approaches. A lesbian approach with aggressive overtones in a prison for women, for example, puts the target in a female role, the one in which she expects to be. In male prisons, however, the male target is put in a female role. This shocks most men. Viewing themselves as "male," they react sharply and often violently when others fail to support the sexual role they see themselves as playing. While not as grave as in male prisons, sexual abuse is still reported as occurring in female prisons. Martin R. Gardner (1975) writes about two female prisoners, charged with escape, who proved their innocence by claiming they had to escape to avoid sexual harassment from other inmates. James Fox, investigating prisoner subculture at New York State's institution for females, Bedford Hills, tells of an incident where sexual aggression was employed by a group to humiliate a female prisoner (personal communication, 1975).

Other reports contain charges of male staff abusing female prisoners. A female prisoner at the Ray Brook Rehabilitation Center, in northern New York State, claimed sexual pressure came from male employees (New York Times, 1975b). In the widely publicized Joan Little case, a female prisoner in the Beaufort County Jail in North Carolina charged she was forcibly accosted by a male guard (New York Times, 1974b).

Just as virtually all sexual aggression in free society is caused by men (Nettler, 1978), so is the problem in prison more acute in male institutions than in female ones. This conclusion is highlighted by the controversy surrounding "Born Innocent," a TV movie about a girl assaulted by other girls in a juvenile institution. The Lesbian Feminist Liberation pressured to have the show dropped, claiming it "has nothing to do with reality. . . .Men rape, women don't" (*New York Times*, 1975a).

Over the years, the literature on crime and corrections has documented the prevalence of sexual aggression among male prisoners. *Scottsboro Boy* (Patterson and Conrad, 1950), for example, describes the experience of a young man who entered a Southern prison several decades ago. In this prison, aggressors ("wolves") were apparently allowed free rein, and then forced weaker men to be their "gal boys." According to the author, virtually all convicts were caught up in this destructive behavior that involved savage exploitation of weaker inmates and could be viewed as the major cause of violence in the prison.

Other sources document similar pictures. The protagonist in *The Jack Roller* (Shaw, 1966), an early classic in criminology, talks about sexual aggression in a reform school to which young men were sent in the 1920s. Sociologists, such as Sykes (1971), in the 1950s found sexual aggression in the institutions they studied, and psychiatrists and other professionals working in prisons have also noted its occurrence (Clemmer, 1958; Huffman, 1960; Karpman, 1948; Roth, 1971). Books about notorious criminals add to this picture. For example, Vincent Bugliosi (1974), in *Helter Skelter*, writes about Charles Manson. As a 17-year-old federal prisoner in the Natural Bridge Camp, Manson held a razor blade to a youth's throat while he sodomized him. Losing 97 days of good time for this act, Manson was transferred to the Federal Penitentiary at Petersburg, Virginia. Within the next eight months, Manson, who later was to leave prison and become a pimp and a murderer, sexually attacked three other prisoners.

Sexual aggression is described in prisons outside the United States. S. P. Srivastava (1974), who wrote his Ph.D. dissertation about an Indian prison, discusses sexual exploitation in an institution in Uttar Pradesh. Aggressors, or *laundbaajs*, in this prison coerced "boyish young newcomers." They used subtle tricks as well as outright force and openly bragged about their exploits. Victims underwent a miserable defamation process.

Former prisoners have also written about sexual agression (Thomas, 1967; Teresa, 1973). Especially interesting among these personal writings are the accounts of conscientious objectors who served time during the Vietnam War. These articulate and literate draft resisters were in a high-risk category for victimization because they were young, middle-class, and white. Bob Martin, for example, an active Quaker and journalist, was put in a Washington, D.C., jail following an antiwar action. Here, he was beaten and forcibly raped about 60 times (Martin et al., 1974).

David Miller, a conscientious objector serving time in the federal system, was transferred from the Allenwood Camp to the maximum security penitentiary at Lewisburg, Pennsylvania. There, Miller became the target of sexual aggressors who offered him gifts and protection in exchange for compliance. As Miller resisted, the aggressors became more forceful. As a believer in nonviolence, Miller refused to use force to protect himself. As a result, he found going to the "hole" the only way he had of solving his problem. After leaving prison, Miller wrote about his experiences. His book, a guide for draft resisters going to prison, deals particularly well with the dilemma of the target committed to nonviolence (Miller and Levy, 1970).

In contrast to the middle-class conscientious objectors' stance toward unwanted sexual advances is Piri Thomas' advice to his nephew, a New York City Puerto Rican entering Great Meadow Correctional Facility (Thomas, 1967):

> Well, the first time he says something to you or looks wrong at you, have a piece of pipe or a good heavy piece of two-by-four. Don't say a damn thing to him, just get that heavy wasting material and walk right up to him and bash out his face and keep bashing 'til he's down and out, and yell loud and clear for all the other cons to hear you. "Mother Fucker, I'm a man I came in here a mother-fucking man. Next time I'll kill you." (p. 256)

The best known investigation of prison rape is the work of Davis (1968b). This inquiry was commissioned by the Philadelphia Police Department and court system in 1968, and it serves as an example of the seriousness of the rape problem where aggressors congregate and officials do not adequately protect vulnerable prisoners. The Philadelphia report estimates that of 60,000 inmates going through the city's system in a 26-month period, 2000 men were subject to sexual assaults. Davis warned at the time that "virtually every slightly built young man committed by the courts is sexually approached within hours after his admission to prison" (p. 3).

The Philadelphia report has received wide publicity, and the city has used its findings to reform its prison system. The question remains, of course, as to how many similar situations may exist elsewhere in the country. Sections of the Philadelphia report are reproduced in numerous books and articles, and some commentators (e.g., Weiss and Friar, 1975) allege that the rape rate described in the Philadelphia report applies generally to other penal settings, including New York's prisons. As we have seen, data fail to support this claim.

Only a few other research studies give any sound data on the incidence of prison sexual aggression. Bartollas et al. (1976) estimated that 16 of 149 boys in an Ohio training school were being sexually exploited at the time of their research in the mid-1970s. Fuller et al. (1976) estimated the sexual assault rate in 1976 for the North Carolina Prison system as less than one percent, based on 30–31 incidents of sexual assault yearly among a population of 4495. Little else is known about nationwide rates of prison rape. No estimates exist for the percentages of prisoners who have been targets of aggressors according to the extended definition of sexual aggression used in this book, which is our next topic.

SCOPE OF THE INQUIRY

This study is limited to sexual behavior perceived as threatening and offensive by targets of aggressors. I look at a continuum of actions, all perceived as aggressive, ranging from verbal propositions to gang rapes. Consequently, the boundaries of my inquiry are set by the men to whom the behavior constitutes a psychologically tangible problem. In this research, men defined themselves as "victims." Strict legal categories, based on objective acts, were secondary to the mental or physical harm actually suffered by targets of aggressors.

In the modern prison, where custody administrators apply contemporary standards of inmate security, incidents of sexual assault are likely to be low, relative to institutions where inmate security is neglected. The problem of sexual aggression, however, does not end simply by making vulnerable individuals physically secure. Events recorded in this book occurred in a prison system that was thought to have a "low" rate of sexual assault. In this setting, single cells are mandated by state law. Well trained staff carry out effective custodial measures. Yet, sexual aggression continues to be a problem, as it can be in the most "professional" of prisons. Extending the definition of sexual aggression beyond rape means that we are discussing a matter not likely to disappear as the trend toward modernization of prison systems continues.

The words defined below, used throughout this book, apply this broadened concept of sexual aggression.

Sexual Aggression: behavior that leads a man to feel that he is the target of aggressive sexual intentions. The perception of the target becomes just as important as the objective actions of the aggressor in defining the situation. Sexual aggression can be viewed as a continuum marked by different levels of force: One end of the continuum might be a target imagining aggression from an aggressor's overture; the other end, the gang rape.

Aggressor: the prisoner who initiates the incident.

Target: the recipient of an approach perceived as aggressive. Some targets are victims of rapes; others flee when confronted with talk of sex. Most targets encounter some form of violence or verbal threat. Others, however, create a fearful situation from stimuli not definable as threatening by objective indices. I consider all of these men "targets."

Sexual Assault: forcible oral or anal sodomy.

Proposition: request for sex that is not accompanied by force or threats.

The idea of sexual approaches being defined as "aggressive" from the perspective of the target involved can be illustrated by the following interview excerpt, which is also a good illustration of the interview style used in this research. The prisoner speaking, let us call him "Dave," is a 24-year-old white man from Utica, New York with an eighth grade education. He was sentenced to prison for setting his own house on fire. He began his confinement awaiting sentencing in the Oneida County jail, where he was a target of sexual approaches. Then, over the next two years, he became a sex target in Auburn, Attica, and Matteawan State hospital, the places where he served out his state prison sentence. I interviewed Dave in the mental health unit of Attica's hospital. (A helpful psychiatric nurse, concerned about my study, had assigned to me a comfortable private interview room.) Dave was a thin, fair, nervous man. He explained to me that prisoners thought he was a "fag" because his nervous condition caused him to appear effeminate. Dave describes how a significant psychological impact can evolve from an almost benign-appearing sexual approach. The event described by Dave occurred in the Oneida County jail:

DAVE: A couple of days later, he approached me again and told me that he would like to have sex with me. And I told him that I wasn't interested in that and that I was married and that I wasn't interested in that. And he somehow resented it. He didn't physically attack me or anything but I told the officer that I wanted to be moved out of that block because of the homosexuals in that block.

I: So when this happened it must have been a pretty tough experience for you? The very first time you are down and then you get a bad vibration from this guy?

DAVE: Yeah.

I: After this happened and before you were transferred, what kind of thoughts went through your mind?

DAVE: Well, the thought that went through my mind was the reason I asked to be moved. My rejecting this individual, what he was liable to do since he was a convicted murderer—waiting trial for murder—what he was liable to do to me. Mostly I was more scared than anything.

I: You had some feelings of fear?

DAVE: Right. And I couldn't understand how he could think this way when the man had just started doing time himself and was married himself. And lots of things went through my mind and then I started to wonder, "Well, if it was like this in, say, the county jail," I started to think, "well, what is it going to be like in prison?" You know, what kind of experiences like that am I going to have to go through in prison. And this bothered me mentally. I never discussed it with my wife or my mother or anything because they get too emotional and I figured that there was really nothing they could do. It made me quite nervous and mostly scared of this person. Why did this individual pick me among, you know, 15 other people? I really didn't know what to do. And the guy—he just kept on pushing the issue and, when I say mentally, I had already come in with mental problems into the jail already because I wasn't sure that I had committed the crime or not and this also bothered me. I was very suspicious. I still am. I know that it is not paranoia because there are a lot of men here that carry weapons and will use them on you and you have to at all times when your back is turned watch yourself because you can get stabbed very easily.

It is clear that Dave's feelings of fear led to anxiety, for he insisted, "This bothered me mentally." He also altered his life-style as a result of the incident, saying, "I told the officer that I wanted to be moved out of that block." These troubles combined with preexisting concerns, for he said he had already come in with mental problems. Themes such as these—anxiety and life-style changes—were analyzed and counted in over 100 interviews held with similar targets of aggressors. To explain this procedure further, I will now explain the methodology employed in this study.

METHODS

Target Study

Most of the men I interviewed were in three New York State Prisons: Attica, Auburn, and Coxsackie. Here, I obtained descriptions of incidents occurring in juvenile institutions, jails, adult prisons or reformatories, and correctional mental health facilities. Interviews were tape-recorded and transcribed. They were open-ended but included all topics listed below:

1. Description of sexual overtures.
2. Description of the physical and verbal response of the person receiving the overture.
3. Description of the thoughts and feelings of the target.
4. Description of living patterns that have resulted from sex pressure.
5. Descriptions of peer and staff interventions.
6. Prisoners' ideas about solutions to their problem.
7. Relationship of sexual pressure to other problems.

Interviews were anonymous and are identified by code numbers. Prisoners were instructed to use no names of other prisoners during the interviews. If any names appeared on the tapes, they were not transcribed. The names appearing in the quotations in this book have been fabricated. Prisoners were not asked to refer to other prisoners. The specific content of interviews was discussed only with immediate members of the research project. Inmates were told that their participation in the study was voluntary and that their participation might help other men in the future, but that their participation would not offer them aid or relief.

In all, I interviewed 107 targets. They came from the following sources:

1. Key prison staff, charged with handling inmate crises, referred 34 targets of aggressors to me.
2. I interviewed at random four percent of the population of Attica and Coxsackie, talking with every 22nd man on the "housing list." Since about a quarter of these men had been involved in incidents of sexual violence, I located 34 targets through this random survey.
3. Targets of sexual aggression tend to congregate in special cell blocks set up to protect vulnerable prisoners. Interviewing all of the men living in such settings in Attica, Auburn, Coxsackie, and Comstock, I located 39 additional targets.

Interviews were conducted from October 1974 to September 1975. On the average, incidents occurred six months before the interview date, although, indeed, some occurred years before the time they were recorded. Others took place only a few days before I spoke to the men. Following the interviews, background data was collected from institutional files.

A "nontarget" control group was selected, made up of four percent of the populations of Attica, an adult prison, and Coxsackie, a youth prison. Men were designated "nontargets" by means of a probing personal interview. The nontarget control group held 59 men.

Aggressor Study

Although the names of 45 aggressors were acquired in several different ways, most of these men were participants in the incidents described by targets. The aggressor group, thus, is primarily made up of the actual players in the interactions examined. On the other hand, it is not representative. Every available aggressor was added to the group because this was the only possible way to obtain a group of these men.

Acquiring an aggressor sample was a sensitive undertaking. In no case were targets asked the names of the men who had been abusing them. In fact, as we have seen, all informants were specifically told not to mention definite names. The ability to work successfully would have been hampered if the word got around that we were trying to get inmates to inform on fellow inmates. Moreover, prisoner informants could have been harmed.

Fortunately, as the target study progressed, I learned some aggressive incidents were recorded by staff in the file of the target or in the file of the aggressor. These files became the main source of the aggressor sample. Since I was gathering prerecorded information, my status as observer of this sensitive activity was maintained. I was not in a likely position to damage either targets or aggressors.

Staff investigations, thus, identified most of the aggressors. In these cases, a correctional officer or administrator prepares a handwritten report. A carbon copy of this report is placed in the file of both target and aggressor. When the interview with the target confirmed the information in the report, the aggressor was added to the research sample. Here are examples of such reports.

Lieutenant's Report: Inmate Brown, C Block Porter, denies any involvement or knowledge of alleged incident. I had Figliani observe inmate through the door and he identified Brown. I then brought Figliani into this office where he identified Brown, in person, as one of the attackers.

Ward 16 Incident Report: Patient Heller and patient Marchland were involved in an altercation in the ward library . . . it seems to stem from possible homosexual advances made by Marchland toward Heller.

Marchland received an injury to his lower lip and a laceration of upper left arm that required eight sutures . . . two screw drivers and a comb with a razor blade taped to it were found.

Heller was placed in camisole for protection of self and others. Marchland confronted Heller and let out with a barrage of threatening statements: "You're a punk kid. I'm going to get you; it might take years, but walk slow and think fast. You went for my throat twice with that blade and missed both times."

Aggressors were generally reluctant to talk about their own personal sexually aggressive behavior and the group exhibited an unusually high refusal rate (30 percent). However, a few interviews did yield rich material from the aggressor's point of view. Unfortunately, these are too few cases to construct any systematic analysis based on interview content. Thus, these interviews serve only as a source of insight into individual aggressor experiences and attitudes.

On certain background variables, aggressors and targets are compared to the characteristics of the entire prison population. Figures used for this comparison have been compiled by State authorities for general purposes. They were made available to us through the courtesy of the New York State Department of Correctional Services.

The first aggressor file was examined in November 1974, the last in December 1975. The first aggressor interview was in January 1975, the last was in October 1975. Files of aggressors were examined in two adult prisons (Attica and Auburn), one youth prison (Coxsackie) and the central files of the Department of Correctional Services. Interviews with aggressors were held in Attica and Coxsackie. The incidents that caused these men to be identified as aggressors occurred in one jail and five prisons throughout New York State. The incidents took place between 1973 and 1975.

Staff Study

Top administrators in Attica, Comstock, Coxsackie, and Auburn were interviewed. In these prisons, mental health professionals were interviewed, along with the counselors and officers responsible for men in protective environments. Additional officers, counselors, sergeants, and lieutenants were interviewed on an unsystematic basis throughout the state. Most of these staff members made decisions about targets or potential targets. Some of these interviews were tape-recorded and transcribed. In other cases, only field notes were taken. Staff comments in regard to the perception and handling of specific cases were also copied out of target's files. These, along with interview content from staff and targets, give us a record of staff-in-action.

Data Analysis

I carried out computer analysis, using two units of study: the individual and the incident. Each unit had its own computer file. Target background information was included in each coded incident, enabling me to correlate background with incident behavior.

In the interviews, I asked men to describe incidents of sexual aggression, encouraging a description of the behavioral moves in the incident. I asked for the words the aggressor said to the target and the words the target said to the aggressor. From interview transcriptions, we made a diagram of each incident, showing the sequence of aggressor and target moves. For example, here is an incident occurring in Auburn, reported to us by Dave, the prisoner from Utica from whose interview we have already quoted:

Aggressor	*Target*
Propositions target in cell block	Refuses politely
Propositions continue	Polite refusals continue
Propositions target	Target locks himself in, refuses to go to work or meals. Tells staff about the problem. Is keeplocked by the adjustment committee for a week, for refusing to work. No staff action against aggressor, who is not told by target the reason for the keeplock. Target moves to different cell block.
Threatens to harm target unless he goes with him (in the yard).	Target informs staff of threat. Is locked up for his protection. Aggressor is locked up for one day. Target transfers to Attica.

In addition to the physical aspects of the incident, a wide range of psychological reactions was reported in these open-ended interviews. We coded and tabulated these responses. Results, however, should be considered with caution. While emotional reactions outline the range of target responses, the frequencies themselves may be suspect. Some targets obstinately refused to discuss their emotions, and questions about feelings were answered by masculine braggadocio, in spite of attempts to break through the poses prison life encourages men to adapt. In other interviews, the degree of rapport required to have men talk freely about their deep and personal feelings was absent. Because of these reasons, there is a likely chance of underreporting of emotional reactions in our survey.

In conclusion, this research is a social psychological examination of a social problem. Our choice of topic and our definitions come from the concerns of troubled men. Our methods and our view of research come from different academic fields. While focusing on the specific issue of sexual violence among male prisoners, our work relates to the general areas of victimization, violence, and "corrections."

The Shape of Victimization

 In this chapter, objective characteristics of incident participants and of incidents themselves are presented. Events reported by targets, tape-recorded and transcribed, were carefully dissected. With the aid of a computer, their characteristics were put in categories and counted. In all, 107 targets furnished 152 incident descriptions. The personal characteristics of these targets, along with those of the aggressors I was able to locate, were also analyzed by computer. In order to predict the type of prisoner most likely to be victimized, targets were statistically compared to nontargets. The significance of this factual portrait is twofold. First, by looking at incident characteristics, we can observe the physical behavior that causes the psychological effects described in later chapters, and we can see the varieties of outward behavior I define as sexually aggressive. Second, by looking at participants' characteristics, we learn about victim potential—a first step toward victim protection.

THE RATE

Choosing 89 men at random from the housing lists of Coxsackie and Attica (about four percent of the total population), I conducted an interview with the men wishing to participate (15 percent declined). On the basis of this interview, 28 percent were classified as having been the targets of sexual aggressors at some time in their institutional custody. To estimate the target rate among the population that was most at risk, I interviewed 23 white youths in Coxsackie during 1975. Seventy-one percent of these white prisoners between the ages of 16 and 21 had been targets of sexual aggression at one time during their confinement. (In comparison to a rate of 28 percent for *all* prisoners.)

Although the random survey indicated that 28 percent of all prisoners interviewed had been targets of aggressors to some degree, only one had been the actual victim of a sexual assault. A probing personal interview conducted with each inmate in the sample lessened the chances of underreporting. The relatively low rate of sexual assault is also suggested by the number of incidents reported by informants as occurring in the two prisons while I worked there. According to staff and prisoners, in the adult prison, with a resident population of about 2000, one or two sexual assaults occurred in a year. Such assaults were somewhat more common in the youth prison of 700, where sexual assault occurred about once every two months during the year I worked there.

INCIDENT CHARACTERISTICS

We divided aggressive overtures into categories that indicate what happened to targets (see Table 2.1). These categories derive from objective characteristics of incidents, i.e., from the words and actions of aggressors. What they describe are aggressive behaviors that trigger psychological responses we will examine later in this book.

The behavior summarized in the table is considered to be aggressive, not because of anything in the behavior itself, but

Table 2.1. Aggressive Behavior in Incidents

Most Severe Behavior in Incident	Number of Incidents in Which Behavior Occurs	Percentage of Total Incidents
Sexual assault	12	8
Other physical violence	39	27
Insulting or threatening language	29	20
Touching or grabbing	11	7
Propositioning only	49	33
Other	8	5
Total	148	100

because it resulted in psychologically tangible harm. This harm was detected through interviews with targets.

As Table 2.1 shows, a third of the targets were physically harmed: They were sexually assaulted, beaten up, or otherwise attacked. In the rest of the encounters, men were subjected to what Goffman (1961) calls "interpersonal contamination." As we see by these examples, sexual overtures can violate "territories of the self" in a number of different ways:

C2-47: Well, you see, we walk through lines and we come down through the mess hall or something like that. The other lines will be standing there and waiting to go up and they will be grabbing at the homosexuals and the weak ones. They will grab their buttocks and feel them up in the buttocks.

* * *

ARE-4: One time I was scrubbing the counter and he happened to come by and patted me on my butt. And I didn't even know it was him. Whoever did it was behind me. I don't play around, because I don't want anyone touching me and I don't touch anyone. That was a frontal attack. If I had something else in my hand other than that wet rag, I don't know what would have happened.

My first encounter was the stare and I realized that some-one was constantly looking at me. No matter where I looked there were his eyes. Then I noticed that he was con-stantly putting his hands on me, this first individual, you know, kind of scratching my elbow when we were walking, kind of touching me when all of us were together in a group, not in formation or anything, but to mess hall where I was working and I would feel a scratching on my elbow. He kept putting his hands on me and he was touching my shoulder and arm, patting my hand and constantly around, ridiculous crap. But enough so that it would be aggravating.

Aggressors, lacking verbal skills and not wanting to incriminate themselves by an overt forceful move, may communicate intentions through touching. Targets are left to interpret and distort these moves. Some aggressors may approach targets by sitting close to them, say, in church, and rubbing their legs against the targets'. When this occurs, the aggressor is protected from accusations of wrongdoing because he can claim the contact was accidental. Inci-dents beginning with casual touching often escalate over time to heightened levels of physical contact. Leg rubbing might be followed by an arm casually thrown around the shoulder of the target, to be interpreted as a friendly action should trouble result. Unless the target reacts assertively to the arm around the shoulder, it may be followed by more explicit and more forceful gestures.

Aggressors direct remarks to targets that are ostensibly seductive but are also abusive and insulting. Commonly, these remarks tell the target that he is understood to be a desirable sex object. Men who have customarily viewed themselves as heterosexual find these remarks predictably dismaying.

C2-27: When they would first start saying things to me, like, "Hey, baby," I would expect to see a secretary walking by or something, I just could not believe that a male would be saying those kind of things to me. And I looked around and wondered what he was looking for or looking at. And I thought the guy must be goofing on me or something, playing a joke. And I then knew after a while that if the guy had a chance he would want to kiss me and have sex with me. Which is something you say to yourself, "This can't be true."

* * *

AR-10: The minute I walked in there was this uproar. They [inmates] hollered obscenities and all sorts of names. They [officers] told me to walk down the middle of this line like I was on exhibition. I was shaking in my boots. They were screaming things like, "That is for me," and "This one won't take long, he will be easy." And, "Look at her eyes." I had no idea of what to do with that. I was scared. I didn't talk to anyone for a while.

When one knows he is attractive to other men, one also knows he is vulnerable to sexual attack. Thus, sexual remarks, such as the following taken from interview transcriptions, cause anxiety:

"You are cute."

"Damn, you're a pretty white."

"Well, you are a fine-looking dude."

"I want you to be my kid."

"I want your ass."

"I want you bad."

"I would like to make you my kid."

Violence and Threats

Fifty-one percent of the incidents contained physical violence. Table 2.2 shows the levels of violence deployed in these incidents. Because most of these events occurred in supervised locations, physical encounters were, for the most part, brief. Nonetheless, at least half of the violent incidents involved fairly high levels of force, i.e., sexual assault, stabbing, clubbing, or beating. Although officers broke up most fights quickly, there were still substantial injuries suffered: Some men were raped; others had wounds inflicted by "shanks" (improvised knives) or "pipes" (any hard object used as a club). Some had bones broken or teeth knocked out.

A prisoner doing time in New York's Great Meadow Correctional Facility described how he killed an aggressor when he was incarcerated in the South several years ago. The target, 16 years old at the time, smashed the aggressor with a chair when the aggressor turned away. Like Billy Budd in Melville's story, the target stuttered: He was agitated by the proposition, and struck out in rage when his speech blocked. Although the incident is anomalous in its amount of violence, it is typical in other respects and illustrates that violence can come from targets as well as aggressors. The incident also shows that the intensity of reactions to aggressors can depend as much on targets' personalities as on the type of approach they face.

Substantial as some of these physical results are, they only reflect

Table 2.2. Physical Harm in Violent Incidents

Personal Damage[a]	Number	Percent
1. Killed	1	1
2. Sexually assaulted	12	16
3. Stabbed or severely clubbed	7	9
4. Beaten badly (no weapons)	20	26
5. Harmed with improvised weapons	5	7
6. Punched, kicked, tripped, slapped	28	37
7. Face spat in, grabbed	3	4
Total	76	100

[a]Ranked in order of diminishing seriousness.

the intensity of the feelings involved. In prison, intimidation is often subtle, and rage is frequently veiled. While homemade prison weapons abound, handguns are unknown. Readily available medical aid reduces the severity of most injuries. Officers intervene quickly. If this were not the case, injury from sexually inspired violence would be even greater than these findings indicate.

We tabulated the kinds of threat used by aggressors. Verbal threats of sexual assault are the most frequent, accounting for 56 percent of total threats. They include statements such as:

"Are you going to give it up or get it taken off?"

"I want your buttocks and if you don't give it to me, it is going to be taken."

"We are going to fuck you in the ass."

"I am going to fuck you up and take your pussy."

"If you don't give it up, you will get your throat cut easy, I got twenty-five years and I don't give a shit."

"Give it up, Man, or I am going to take it right here and kill you."

"Look, Man, I have got a knife and we want to see what you have got."

"If I hear of you giving it out, then, with anyone else in this institution, not only am I going to fuck you, I will make you suck my dick, and I will beat your head right into the ground."

"Well, if you want to be a dirty bitch, we got to take this pussy."

"You're going to play what I want you to play."

"What would you do if I just took it and if I pulled your pants down and just took it?"

"I'll play it rough with you and then after you break, you'll be mine."

Aggressors use all kinds of other threats, often promising high levels of force, even death. Regardless of the aggressors' intent, the target who takes these threats at face value receives the impression that he is in a life-threatening situation. For example, aggressors told targets the following:

"I am going to cut you up."

"You are dead."

"Look, you tell anybody what I told you and I am going to stick a knife in your heart."

"If you call the C.O., we will kill you."

"If I find out that you are gay, then I'm going to kill you for not participating with me."

Duration

About half of the incidents were single episodes lasting less than two hours (some of these only a few minutes). Brief incidents were often terminated by assertive gestures by targets:

ARE-4: This black man was looking over towards me and I had no idea what he had in mind so I was continuing with the pinochle game. Every once in a while I would hear a remark, "Hi, cutie," or something of this nature. And then he would smack his lips. This guy began to be annoying after a while. He kept it up and I finally realized that it was I that he was insinuating his remarks to.

And so I finally laid my cards down and went over to him and said, "You're disgusting. Do you get any enjoyment out of that?"

And his exact words were, "I'm going to get into your ass."

And I told him right out, "It's going to be a cold day in hell before you ever think about it."

He said, "If I have to, I'll hit you over the head and take it that way."

And I said right then and there, "That's the only way you're ever going to get anything like that from me."

And since that there has been no recurrence and he has never come back.

* * *

C2-28: Well, they leave your cells open all the day in E Block. This guy came in and he came into my cell. And the officer was getting medication or something. And there was no one in the ward at all. And when he came in he started jumping on me and started taking my pants off. And I just started beating the hell out of him. His face was all bloody and everything. And then I went out and I said, "Hey, get this guy out of here!" I hollered to the officer. I told him to get this guy out of here and that he was crazy. And that was the only episode that happened in there.

About a quarter of the incidents extended past two days, many of these lasted up to two weeks in duration. Such transactions were marked by a number of episodes, none serving to end absolutely the aggressor's pursuit of a particular target. In some long incidents, aggressors become hopelessly infatuated with targets. A volcano builds when these emotions are unreciprocated. Their overtures rejected, these aggressors become violent because they are snubbed. Targets can also be violent in these cases when the tension from the aggravating situation accumulates over time until they explode. As we see by this example, some aggressors seem unwilling or unable to give up their intense attachment for individual targets.

ARE-2: I said, "You're beginning to make me hate you." And there was nothing I could do about it. And then he started asking about me. And he said in due time I would like him. I might say something to him and then he says something to me and I don't respond to him. Like he might say something like, "Are you ready?" And I don't react to him. I just say, "I despise you." And he takes it as a joke.

He said he wouldn't mess with me no more. And I felt good. And the next day he said, "Come to the yard."

And I said, "What the fuck is wrong with this guy?"

He has told me about four times that he wants to leave me alone. And each time he says, "I can't do it. I can't do it."

Other incidents take place over time because physical barriers block aggressors from directly reaching targets. They have to deliver threats verbally, through bars or across corridors, at whatever chance moments their patrolled, iron-grilled world permits. Some aggressors, during this time, may try to put fear in targets, hoping to coerce them to go willingly to private locations where sex can take place. Some targets, locked in physical safety, become like animals tormented in cages, never knowing when a persecutor will appear before their cell door.

C2-18: Well, just about every time that we were locked up for breakfast and stuff like that, they would come around my cell and say that they were going to get me as soon as the C.O. was not around.

I: And what were you saying to them?

C2-18: I was just saying that they would have to kill me first.

I: And what did they say?

C2-18: They just said that they would knock me out and take it. And I would say that they would have to knock me out or kill me before I would give it up.

I: So how many times did this happen that you were in your cell and they were out there talking to you?

C2-18: Just about every day—for about two weeks.

High-Risk Times and Places

Eighty-seven percent of the 152 sexual incidents described occurred in state institutions for adult offenders. The remainder took place in jails or juvenile facilities. Since only adult male prisoners were interviewed, we should perhaps expect to find incidents concentrated in state prisons. However, we should also note that most prisoners spend at least some time in jails before they end up as long-term residents of maximum security penitentiaries. Thus, the finding of few incidents occurring in jails in this study may be taken as evidence that the intensity of sexual aggression in New York State is far higher in state prisons than it is in county jails within the state. As we will see later, a partial requisite of sexual aggression is cultural *heterogeneity*. To the degree that local county jails in New York State are culturally *homogeneous*, their prisoners avoid sexual aggression.

Among the incidents taking place in state prisons, 77 percent occurred within 16 weeks after the target entered the state penal system. This makes the "reception center" (a separate prison where new men are diagnosed and oriented) and the first transfer prison (where men go after reception) the most risky stages of confinement.

Before they became targets of sexual aggression, most men had experience in confinement. Sixty-five percent, for example, had served previous terms in juvenile or adult institutions. Looking at the amount of time served by targets, we find that almost three-quarters of them served six months or more prior to the time of their victimizing incident. Clearly, the prison sex target should not be thought of as a naïve first offender. Likewise, institutional experience alone failed to make a man immune from aggressive sexual approaches.

Since targets, on the average, come into prison with as much incarceration experience behind them as do nontargets, an important variable relating to target selection has to do with the amount of time spent in the actual prison (or prison system) where the incident occurs. Newness in the social setting marks one for testing, regardless of experience in similar settings. Aggressors primarily select new men for targets, hoping to find them either weak or willing, or so inexperienced as to be easily swayed. To an inquiring aggressor, the response to a sexual approach can categorize a new man as "available" or "unavailable" for sexual activity. Moreover, since the lonely victim is seen as easy prey, some new men attract aggressors because "new jacks" are less likely than others to have found acceptance in established prison cliques. Because he has yet to define his identity to others and because his lack of peer support marks him as weak, the new prisoner is in a high-risk group for sexual victimization.

Some men have incidents after the first 16 weeks. In many of these cases, they have failed to develop a prison life-style deterring sexual approaches. They may have been involved in incidents where responses failed to inspire respect. They may have failed to join groups or failed to get themselves installed in jobs or cell blocks offering protection. Failing to cope with sexual aggression during the first months of prison may make some men vulnerable during the months that follow. A few prisoners who fail to resolve the problem in these first few months may find themselves with a public image encouraging sexual approaches. A minority of targets throughout their confinement are seen as weak because they cannot fight, or as feminine because other men are attracted to them. They are likely to be approached at any time until their release.

While incarceration experience itself has little to do with a man being selected to be a target, it does affect his reaction to aggressive overtures. An experienced convict, knowing the risks of a weak public image, having already been socialized into the violent prison subculture, is more likely than the "new jack" to respond with force when approached. For example, this prisoner, who served five years in Massachusetts before finding himself in a reception center in

New York, tells how he reacted when approached a few days after entering Sing Sing:

AR-7: I was out in the reception company and every night I would pass the water out and you would make a lot of conversation. So this dude come over and he asked me if I was homosexual, you know, and I said it was none of his business. It went on for about a week and a half and finally he came up and said, "I want you to take care of this thing." So I didn't pay no attention and he just whipped it out and put it on my buttocks and he said, "You are either going to do something now or get the money out that you owe me." So I just poured the bucket of hot water on him. He didn't have no shirt on or nothing and his fly was open, so I just picked up the bucket of water and threw it on him.

The places where incidents occur also provide clues for preventing potential harm. Moreover, since most aggressors were violent criminals on the street, knowing the place of incidents has significance for understanding the ecology of violent crime in general. We know that rape (and other violent crime) tends to occur most often in areas close to the neighborhoods where the offenders live (Schafer, 1977; Amir, 1971). This argues for increasing social defense in any location marked by the social characteristics of violent offenders.

Similarly, in prison, aggressors tend to victimize those within their immediate proximity. Thus, over half of the incidents of prison sexual aggression in this study took place in the living quarters of the men involved. Since New York State prisons generally give every man a single cell, most of these events took place in public areas, primarily galleries in front of cells and shower and toilet rooms. Single cells, for the most part, gave men protected living space so long as they were locked in. On the other hand, an institution for insane criminals within the state housed men in dormitories. Here, according to interviews with former prisoners of this hospital, the level of sexual aggression in living quarters appears to have rivaled at times the rampant and open victimization reported as occurring at one time in the open prison dormitories of Arkansas (*Holt vs Sarver*, 1971) or Philadelphia (Davis, 1968a,b).

Surprisingly, 16 percent of the incidents occurred in prison shops or schoolrooms, areas generally under the eyes of direct supervision. Because of staff presence, however, most of these incidents fell short of rape and many did not even generate disciplinary infractions. By whispering threats and furtively gesturing, experienced sexual aggressors can operate in the most secure of settings. Just as the convict moonshiner persists in making home brew, in spite of the presence of guards and work supervisors, the prison "player" carries on his daily hustle for sexual activity.

CHARACTERISTICS OF PARTICIPANTS

Age

In our sample, targets and aggressors are approximately the same age, while nontargets tend to be older than both. Since sexual aggression was most prevalent in the youth institution, the closeness in age between targets and aggressors reflects sampling procedures more than the way aggressors select targets. Since the prison system was segregated by age, generally only youthful targets were available to youthful aggressors. Where age groups were more mixed, however, researchers have found targets to be younger than aggressors (Davis, 1968a,b). However, since sexual aggression is most concentrated among young people, separating youths from adults does not solve the problem. Youth is associated with all types of violence, not only sexual exploitation (Wolfgang and Ferricuti, 1967). Thus, over 60 percent of targets and aggressors were under 21.

Aggressive youths prey on those around them whom they perceive to be weak and attractive targets. Placing such young aggressors in prison fails to reduce their criminal behavior. Whereas before they may have mugged elderly citizens in the street, they now, while incarcerated, select other youths as sex targets. This makes sexual aggression most intense among youthful prisoners. Until such time as effective measures for treating youthful violence are developed, we may expect to encounter high levels of sexual victimization in prisons inhabited by young violent offenders.

Ethnicity

The target rate varied considerably by ethnicity. About half of the whites in the random sample were targets at one time, compared to about a fifth of the blacks and Hispanics. If we look only at whites interviewed in the youth prison, the rate is even higher (71 percent), indicating the problem is most severe among white youths. Looking at the race of the aggressors in incidents described by targets, we find that most are black (80 percent), some are Hispanic (14 percent), and a few are white (6 percent). The percentages are almost reversed when we examine the ethnicity of targets in incidents: Most incidents had white targets (83 percent), some had black targets (16 percent), and a few had Hispanic targets (2 percent). Other studies parallel our finding with respect to the tendency of targets to be white and aggressors to be black (Bartollas et al., 1976; Davis, 1968a, b).

Since white inmates in these specific institutions are predominately from upstate New York, while black inmates are drawn more heavily from New York City, it might be conjectured that some of the race differences merely reflect a big-city–small-city difference. However, although targets tend to be associated with small cities and rural areas this association does not continue when we control for race. The white prisoner from New York City is just as likely to have been a target as the white prisoner from other, less densely inhabited, New York State counties.

Interview data indicate whites become targets because they are perceived to be weak and sexually attractive. One reason why sexual aggressors perceive some whites as weak is that young urban blacks see strength in group membership (Johnson, 1976). Those blacks who never become targets tend to explain their invulnerability by reference to group ties. The same men class others as weak when they do not have a group behind them.

AR-45: If you come in here alone then they will try to crack on you for something. But if they know that you know people and that you have been here for awhile, then they know better. They try to pick on some of the weak ones. They like to pick on them.

* * *

CR-11: I don't have all that hassle like all the rest of the new guys that come. You see, I have got a whole lot of homies and the new ones come in, they don't know nobody. That is why they have to go through all that hassle, the dudes talking about ripping them off and all that stuff. You see, after you know somebody then you don't have to worry about it. But they don't know nobody so they have to go through all that hassle. It is mostly the white boys and they get some of the black boys, but not too many of them. If the white dude knows somebody, then the black dude don't mess with him.

* * *

CR-9: Most of the people that they do it to is people that don't
have no friends and they can't fight. They just don't hang
around a lot of people.

* * *

AU-1: You come in here and you don't, like, know anybody, and
finally you see that one guy that you remember from 25
years ago, light years away. Right away you have found a
friend. Until you have found a foothold or something—a
friend that is willing to help you without wanting to impose
upon you—it is a rough situation.

Whites are a minority in the population. Yet, Puerto Ricans, also a
minority, do not tend to be targets. It is not minority status per se
that accounts for the ethnic pattern in this interaction; it is the characteristics of the cultures involved. When blacks and Puerto Ricans
come to prison, they often encounter a group of "home boys" or
"homies" ready to accept them. Some have known these associates
on the street or in the detention centers of New York or some other
large city. The peer group has offered protection (and other opportunities) both in the street and in the institution. Such groups, having their origins in urban slums, are specialized informal organiza-
tions that protect members from exploitation.

Whites in prison also form into groups, but find it harder to do so.
White groups in prison also differ from black groups in that they are
less powerful, less cohesive, and have less potential for violence.
White groups are less likely to retaliate for a slight to one of their
members. White groups also inspire less fear in exploiters. Many
targets some from rural areas, small towns, and small cities. Since
they come from areas of less concentrated criminality, they stand
less chance than do blacks of meeting other prisoners from their
home neighborhoods. Even when white inmates find familiar faces,
these associates are likely to lack both a gang tradition and a violent
tradition. Blacks and Hispanics who come from urban areas with
high violent crime rates tend to find close associates (and often even
relatives) in prison. Whites are less likely to form groups, and the
groups they do form tend to be less adapted than black or Hispanic
groups to violence or its corollary—protection.

Other obstacles may keep some whites isolated, at least for a
while. Social class divides whites in prison more than other factors
(Bartollas et al., 1976). Some middle-class whites disdain lower-class
whites; soft drug offenders view themselves as a counterculture; and
some whites in prison reject other whites because they see them as

criminal deviants. Whites, more than others, are apt to look on fellow prisoners as unsavory, immoral individuals. Some whites in prison see themselves as "normal" and others (including other whites) as "abnormal." Forces acting against white cohesion are important in explaining why whites tend to become targets, for the isolate is seen as "weak" by aggressors.

Aggressors know they will be in trouble if they "mess with" an Hispanic. Latins in prison form close bonds just as they do in their communities. Newly arriving Latin inmates quickly join existing Latin groups. Whites, in comparison, are frequently distant and cold toward newcomers:

AR-42: They [white targets] would come in by themselves and they don't know anyone. You might know this individual but nobody makes a move to call the guy over or clue him in on what is going on. It is hard to make friends in jail. If somebody don't know you, they are not going to go over and just say, "Hi, how are you. I am so-and-so." And when they [aggressors] see the guy alone he is open for this trouble. He is looking for trouble. Someone will go over and hit on him.

A substantial part of prison sexual aggression, like rape on the street (Amir, 1971), can be attributed to aggressors acting together. Multiple aggressors (pairs or groups) carried out almost half of the incidents in this study. However, targets generally handled the physically aggressive aspects of incidents alone. Although many received advice, generally recommending violence against aggressors, in only four cases did peers actively help targets. In part, the absence of aid reflects a prison norm that calls for personal difficulties to be handled individually. The norm holds that if one can surmount tests of manhood unaided, one's manhood is asserted. In addition, aggressors choose loners because such men appear weak, easy to "get over on." Shame and embarrassment also exclude peer support. The target may discuss personal sexual problems with difficulty. He may worry that others, if they know, will see him as a "punk" or a "pussy." In prison, the man attracting sexual advances, even if unwanted, risks becoming labeled a homosexual, a dismaying prospect for the straight prisoner.

Physical Appearance

Targets on the average weighed 15 pounds less than aggressors and 17 pounds less than nontargets. Weight differences increase when we compare white targets to white nontargets. On the average, the white prisoner who avoided becoming a target weighed 20 pounds more than the white target. Slightness, in a prison subculture, is one possible attribute of weakness, though being black or Hispanic, or being white in a group, can cancel out the liability of small size. For the isolated, small size may increase the chance of an aggressor approach.

Prison aggressors look to attractiveness as well as to weakness when they select targets. Attractiveness, in this case, generally means that the potential target resembles a sexually desirable woman.

I: What is it in their being more attractive? When someone has been down for so many months and so many years, what do they look for in a man if they are looking for some man to get over on?

The aggressor: The way he walk. The size of his ass. His facial expressions, his ways and actions. If his face look like a woman, they is going to think that he is a woman. The psychological thing about it is that any dude—white or black dude or any Puerto Rican—can come in here looking like a woman. And you say, "Damn, Man, that man looks like a woman. He had to be squeeze in a certain institution."

As in heterosexual affairs, of course, the ideal sex partner does not always resemble the actual sex partner. Our inquiry located targets who were black as well as white, large as well as small, ugly as well as good-looking. Nonetheless, most informants reported young slender white men were the highest object of desire. To the extent that sexual aggression satisfies status needs, moreover, the white target brings the highest status to the aggressor because peers admire the white prize as a sex object and admire the man who can win him. The young white's appeal lies in his presumed naïveté and his physical appearance, which is perceived as feminine and sexually exciting. The aggressor sees himself as a male; therefore, he selects targets who look, to him, like females. Choosing a member of another race may help this process. The young white target, like the prison queen, is feminized; aggressors even refer to him with female pronouns. Like a woman on the street, he is viewed as an object of masculine exploitation.

AR-12: Well, it had to be the way that he appeared to them physically because he wasn't a bad-looking dude. He looked younger than what he really was and his hair was long. All I can remember about him was that he wasn't the type that was heavy-handed and rough. He wasn't like that. He would rather sit down and play checkers or cards rather than play football or basketball and that is maybe what attracted them to him.

* * *

AR-18: I was trying to understand why was he selected. When he started talking I could understand. Like the way that his voice was—like it sounded tender like he was about to cry. So, like, I told him, it is the way that you carry yourself. You have got smaller guys coming in here and they don't deal with the problem. So it is a way that a man carries himself. Like you can watch a person and tell just about how much he will take before he will break. They have hair like girls and I feel sorry for them, man. They're in big trouble. The girls have long hair and there is something about the dudes that they like and they say, "That looks like a girl to me. Doesn't that look like a girl to you?"

Potential for Violence

In prison, potential for violence is an asset. Prestige results if one can act tough when the situation is defined as calling for it. Those who lack the ability to muster a reaction of power or those who lack a reputation of being capable of violence are apt to be victimized. The attribute is an important criterion when an aggressor selects a target. Approaching some men can result in risk while approaching others carries no risk. The values of the mainstream prison culture call for a violent response to an unsolicited sexual approach. Aggressors, who are members of this "subculture of violence," look for targets who deviate from this norm. As we will see in subsequent chapters, aggressors' expectations are not always met. But aggressors, before making an approach to a target, have an expectation that the target is less likely than others to respond violently, that he has had little experience in dealing with violence.

In interviews, aggressors explain how a potential for violence deters approaches:

AA-13: You see a young pretty dude who doesn't come in here on a violent record. Now, he is probably in the worst situation than the guy that comes in here on a violent record. Because if you know that a guy has murdered someone on the street, and has taken a life, and is in here for life, you are going to think three or four times—not just once but three or four times—before you go up against him.

* * *

AR-3: When they first came in the butch kids would stand by the door and they would watch and wait for all the guys to come in. And they would see them come in from outside the gates. And so they would pick a fight with them. And if the guy would fight, that might stop the butch kids. I wouldn't say that that would end it, but it might put the question in his mind that this was just a fight and then the next time this kid might kill him. And I think that this might put a little bit of pressure on the butch kid and might raise him out a little bit.

* * *

AR-5: Somebody that shows he's timid, who is real quiet. That is basically it. Someone who is real quiet and withdrawn and looks scared. He looks frightened you know. He is most apt to be approached.

In American society, expressions of aggression differ greatly among social classes and ethnic groups (Gold, 1958). In New York State prisons, a higher percentage of blacks than whites are serving time for violent offenses. In addition to being seen as weak because they have no group behind them, whites are also seen as weak because they are less likely than blacks or Latins to respond violently to perceived threats. In our survey, the most extreme violence against perceived threats comes from blacks and Puerto Ricans. In one case, when a man made a sexual request to him, a young black killed the man with a chair. In another case, a Puerto Rican, threatened with sexual assault, gave the aggressor a cut across the face requiring 22 stitches.

Within our data set, one index of "potential for violence" is provided by the nature of past criminal behavior, namely, whether an inmate has a commitment offense that involves personal force or threat of force. An examination of the convictions prior to the current commitment offense reveals that only 25 percent of targets had a conviction for forcible crime in contrast to 58 percent of nontargets and 79 percent of aggressors. An inspection of the nature of the current commitment offense (the crime for which prisoners were serving time when we interviewed them) indicates that force or threat was used by 46 percent of targets, 85 percent of nontargets, and 84 percent of aggressors. Thus, there is a strong association between being a target and having offense histories involving no threat or use of personal force. However, it is important to consider the possible effect of race on these findings.

When the relationship between target status and use of force in the commitment offense is examined for white, black, and Hispanic prisoners separately, these findings reveal that there are only five black or Hispanic prisoners in the "no-force" category, which should make us cautious about generalizing. However, it is interesting to note that four out of the five black and Hispanic nonviolent prisoners are targets. Thus, among blacks and Hispanics there is a tendency for targets to have been committed for a nonforcible offense. Among whites, the relationship is in the same direction but is of small magnitude. Indeed, the control for race results in a considerable reduction in the overall relationship between nonviolent crime and target status. The association between race and target status remains a strong one, regardless of offense history. For example, among violent offenders interviewed, we find 31 of the 40 whites who committed crimes of force are targets, while only 13 of 49 black or Hispanic violent criminals are targets.

Disciplinary Infractions

Both aggressors and targets have higher average numbers of disciplinary infractions than nontargets. This is a function of their younger ages as well as a function of their concentration in the youth prison, where officers are more likely to "write up" an inmate than are officers in the adult prison. Targets also have more *violent* infractions than nontargets (although youths still tend to get more violent reports than adults). This difference *is* tied to target status. The finding of targets having more violent disciplinary infractions than nontargets seems to contradict the assumption that targets are generally less violent than other inmates. However, a large number of targets' violent infractions are fights precipitated by sexual approaches. Targets are involved in prison violence, not because they are more violent than nontargets, but because being a target may involve a violent encounter with an aggressor.

Mental Health Residence

When compared to nontargets, there is an association between being a target and prior mental health residence. This association holds regardless of sampling procedures: Nearly as many randomly selected targets had mental histories as other targets. Similarly, more targets than nontargets were in "special classes" (for the retarded or emotionally disturbed) when in high school. Especially if he has other features characteristic of potential targets, the man with a handicap is likely to be approached for sex because he may be alone in prison. In addition to his weakness, his psychological peculiarities may make it easier for an aggressor to dehumanize him. The odd-acting man, especially if he is young and from an unsophisticated background, may be seen more easily as something less than a man. Exploiting him sexually may also be easier because the probability of empathy is reduced.

CONCLUSION

According to Amir, "rape is ecologically bound." Areas producing high rates of crime against people produce high rates of forcible rape. If such neighborhoods are black, black rapists chose black victims because both live in proximity. They are often acquaintances, at least by sight. Just as the low-income black ghetto in Amir's study has a high rate of rape, so does the youth prison in our study have a high rate of sexually aggressive incidents (most of which fall short of completed rapes because of security measures). Youths from the subculture of violence inhabit both the ghetto and the youth prison: They initiate most sexual aggression in the two settings.

The young black female, living close to rapists, often becomes the victim in the streets. Similarly, the slight white youth, designated a female by the aggressors living close to him, becomes the model target in prison. In the street, social circumstances provide victims to offenders. In prison, common incarceration locks potential targets to aggressors. Prisons with concentrations of violent offenders, youthful members of the subculture of violence, have high levels of sexual aggression—just as in urban ghettos. While some prison sexual aggression, like some heterosexual rape, can occur in any setting, victimization seems to be most prevalent in institutions where urban ghetto culture lives behind the walls. Such is the case, for example, with the prisons of Philadelphia or the jails of Washington, D.C.

Other writers interpret this ethnic pattern as a sign that aggressors aim to humiliate and harm their targets, claiming black prisoners choose white targets in order to get back at all whites for what they have done to blacks. I suggest an alternative explanation (discussed more thoroughly in Chapter 6). I see aggressors choosing white victims for two primary reasons: (1) because whites are seen as weak, and (2) because whites are seen as sexually attractive. The slight, white prisoner, whose physical appearance makes him a more attractive and a weaker target than the heavier inmate of his race, thus is more likely than others to be a target.

Target responses to aggressor overtures reflect participant backgrounds. The typical target is shown to be a lower-class, undereducated youth from rural areas, small towns, and small cities. His culture puts him at a disadvantage when confronted with tough urban blacks. Also, because of his background, he is likely to value highly a masculine image. When he knows aggressors think of him as a "girl" and when he doubts his ability to counteract their threats and/or attacks, the psychological impact can be devastating.

Our statistical findings fail to suggest any easy solutions to this problem. Classification, which would be aimed at separating potential targets from potential aggressors, would have the result of imposing racial segregation on public facilities. Presently, such a move would be contrary to the aim of equal treatment for all races. Increasing security might have little effect, for we have seen how incidents occur even in areas covered by staff; also, we must consider the human costs in calling for the greater repression increased custody implies. The harmful potential effects of such solutions must be balanced against the good they might do. This requires an examination of the psychological severity of the problem, a task we undertake in the forthcoming chapters.

Target Violence

 Most prison violence involves inmates assaulting each other (Cohen et al., 1976). One reason is that violent men and men from violent subcultures live in prison. As violence behind the walls becomes acceptable behavior, prison itself becomes a "subculture of violence" (Conrad, 1966). When otherwise peaceful men live with prisoners who are dangerous or perceived to be dangerous, they become distrustful and fearful. These feelings of vulnerability cause those who have not been violent before to arm themselves and prepare themselves psychologically for fighting. Thus, in prison, sexual aggression results in two main types of violence: (1) Aggressors use violence to intimidate targets, and (2) targets of aggressors react violently to sexual approaches. This chapter examines the latter class of violent behavior, i.e., target violence precipitated by aggressive sexual approaches.

Hans Toch, as a member of the California Task Force on Institutional Violence, constructed a typology of prisoners in violent encounters (Toch, 1965). He calls the man whom I discuss here the "Homosexual Self-Defender." This prisoner, according to Toch, uses violence against men who make sexual approaches to him in order to be left alone. According to Toch, "The effort here is to get out of a corner by eliminating whoever is blocking the exit" (1965).

For example:

> Following a heated altercation between inmates S and L, S obtains a razor blade, enters L's cell, and cuts L about the face and chest. S testifies that L had visited him to involve him in homosexual activities, and had been pressuring him. Other inmate sources point out that S has been under pressure from several homosexuals. (Toch, 1965)

Observers describe similar target reactions in a number of settings (Huffman, 1960; Thomas, 1967). Following the riot of 1971, the New York State Special Commission on Attica (1974) interviewed inmates in Attica, who frequently voiced their belief that violence is the only way to ward off sexual attacks. The Commission noted:

> The irony was not lost on the inmates. They perceived themselves surrounded by walls and gates, and tightly regimented by a myriad of written and unwritten rules; but when they needed protection, they often had to resort to the same skills that had brought many of them to Attica in the first place. (p. 101)

When targets fight aggressors, it reminds us of victim-precipitated homicide (Schultz, 1964). Offenders are incited to assaultive responses by the aggressive actions of their victims. Victims of targets (sexual aggressors), like many homicide victims in the street, often have been previously arrested for crimes of violence. Their patterns of conduct involve them in situations that provoke others to hostile reactions. In prison, a physical environment enforcing contact between antagonists, the probability of an aggressor provoking a violent response may be even greater than in the street. As Albert Cohen points out, prisons create "back-against-the-wall situations" because threatened men often lack the option of withdrawing (Cohen et al., 1976). When interactions contain potential for conflict, confinement itself hastens violence.

A study of violence in six California prisons in 1963 and 1964—one of the few sources classifying inmate assaults—indicates the kinds of contribution that sexual aggression can make to prison violence. The report breaks inmate-to-inmate assaults into the following categories.

Accidental, real, or imagined insult combined with hypersensitivity	35%
Homosexual activities	25%
Pressuring (for possessions)	15%

Racial conflict	12%
Infᴖrmant activities	9%
Retaliation for past assaults	7%

Incidents attributed to homosexuality divide almost equally between homosexual rivalry (12 percent) and homosexual force (13 percent) (Toch, 1965). However, as we shall see in this chapter, it is possible for sexual aggression to play a role in the other categories listed above.

PREVALENCE

I define physical violence to include instances where one person was forcefully touched by another, this being marked by vehement feelings or the aim to injure or abuse. According to such a definition, 51 percent of 150 incidents in my study involved physical violence. About half of these were initiated by aggressors using force against unprovoking targets. Targets began the rest. These were clearcut violent responses to sexual approaches targets perceived as aggressive.

THE VIOLENT TRANSACTION

We followed a method suggested by Toch, who states:

> In this type of approach, each move is seen as the rational response by one player to the play of another. The focus is on logical possibilities left open by preceding moves and on logical implications of each move for successive moves. These possibilities and implications can be conceptualized and qualified (1969, p. 35).

Diagraming 114 transactions (incomplete cases were left out), we grouped them according to the aggressor's first move. They fall into the following four categories:

1. Incidents begun by sexual overtures accompanied by offensive remarks and gestures ($N=42$)
2. Incidents begun by polite propositions ($N=36$)
3. Incidents begun by physical attacks ($N=21$)
4. Incidents begun by verbal threats ($N=15$).

With an examination of the largest group, we see that over half of these transactions, begun by aggressors directing offensive remarks or gestures to targets, quickly escalated to violence. The moves in those sequences culminating in violence commonly follow this pattern:

1. a. Aggressor(s) makes offensive sexual overture.
   b. Target tries to withdraw or target responds with force or threats and a fight starts.
2. a. Aggressor repeats overture, accompanied by threats.
   b. Target uses physical force against aggressor and a fight starts or target answers with counterthreat and a fight starts.

I use an example of this transaction from Coxsackie, a prison housing 700 youths ranging in age from 16 to 21. The target is a white marijuana dealer from Florida. The aggressor is black, a violent offender from New York City. During the incident an officer looks on but is out of earshot:

C2-27: While I was taking a shower he said to me, "You're all right and you're going to be mine later." There was two or three saying it, but they had one spokesman. . . . They were in the shower and they were waiting to have me turn around so that they could see my ass. . . . They were saying that I was going to be theirs and they would take care of me and buy me cigarettes and that I would be their main squeeze.

And I said, "Well, you can see me later, but we're going to fight about it, because you're not going to get anything out of me."

So he said, "Okay, Angel, that's okay, I'll play it rough with you and then after you break then you'll be mine."

So I rinsed off and then I got the fuck out. . . . So I'm over there by the door and as he was going out he put his arm around me and as he did that, I pushed his arm away and I said, "I don't play that, man."

And he said, "Well, you're going to play what I want you to play."

And I said, "Definitely not—I don't want to hassle."

And he said, "You're going to be mine." And he leaned over and said that he was going to whisper something in my ear and I told him to back off, gave him a shove and he came back fighting. I hit him a couple of times and then the

guards broke it up and then we were both locked up for the
same amount of time.

An important feature of this fight is that before the violence, the
target tries to withdraw, but cannot. As he tells us:

C2-27: I figured that he would want to hassle, so I got my clothes
on and I went away from his group of people and then I
went out the door and stayed away from him and I thought
that maybe he would keep away from me that way and go
on to somebody else. And I noticed that he was talking to
some other people and giving them the same thing. I
thought, if he's hassling somebody else, I'm not any hero
and I'm not going to go defend somebody else.

Cornered, his back against the wall, the target starts the fight (i.e.,
by shoving the aggressor)—only after his antagonist has repeatedly
propositioned him, threatened him, and attempted to whisper en-
dearments in his ear. Because prison restricts movement, the trans-
action escalates to violence, even though one of the participants
wants to retreat.

Why does the target finally shove the aggressor, thereby changing
a verbal encounter to a physical one? Mindful that an officer is supervising the shower area, why can't the target limit himself to verbal responses? Whether his reaction springs from panic or the cool
decision to make a preemptive strike, the root cause is fear. Following the aggressor's initial move, the target's thoughts are a mixture
of fear and self-doubt.

C2-27: I was saying, "What could I do if all three of these guys
came and jumped me?" I could probably hit a couple of
them but I'm thinking of all these martial arts that I'm going
to break into and all I've seen is Kung Fu on T.V. And there
was nothing to pick up and I didn't have any shoes that I
could kick them with.

If this target had felt safe, the fight might have been avoided. But
prisons are places of fear where violence feeds on itself and breeds
more violence. If this target had been able to withdraw, the fight
might have been avoided. But prison prohibits free movement and
men in antagonistic transactions lash out when cornered. If the target had been separated from abusive and threatening comments, the

incident would never have occurred. But society deposits its bullies and exploiters in prison. Inevitably, behind the walls, they continue these patterns of behavior, directing their aggression against weaker prisoners instead of free citizens.

Forty-two incidents, like the above example, began with propositions accompanied by offensive remarks or gestures. Twenty-four (or 57 percent) ended in violence. Many incited sharp target reactions from the very first: 12 targets, for example, fought with aggressors immediately following their offensive overtures.

Does target violence work? Or is it senseless, an overreaction to a situation that could be resolved by talking over the problem? To examine this question, let us compare, still within the category of incidents begun by offensive remarks or gestures, targets responding violently to targets trying to ignore or respond politely to these sexual overtures. Only one target who responded without violence succeeded in ending this type of incident. In the other transactions in this category, the nonviolent target response was met in the following ways:

1. Seven aggressors repeated the offensive remark or gesture;
2. Four aggressors leveled sexual threats at targets; and
3. Four aggressors attacked targets.

Polite refusals, thus, tended to encourage aggressors to continue their offensive behavior. We know violent responses to unwanted sexual overtures are normative expectations of the convict community. Unfortunately, in some instances, they may actually be necessary for surviving incarceration with dignity.

We also grouped 36 incidents sequentially that opened with requests for sex—propositions. Twelve of these incidents evolved into physical violence. This escalation usually occurred in one of two ways. In the first, the target replied to the request for sex with a polite refusal, or ignored the request. Following this response, the aggressor reacted violently or accompanied a renewed request with threats. In the second sequence, the target, hearing the request, reacted with the use of force. In one-third of these incidents, targets responded with threats of their own before propositioners made violent or threatening moves. These threats ended half of these incidents, while the others escalated to higher levels of force.

The messages being communicated—that the propositioner wanted sex with the target, and that the target wanted the aggressor to stay away—tended to be confused by threats on both sides. In this scenario, threats often escalated into physical violence. Some targets heard a proposition and snarled back. Others attempted to reason with propositioners and ended up snapping back when their reasoning failed. Aggressors, beginning their approaches with requests for sex, were drawn into conflict for varying reasons. For example, a refusal might suggest the necessity for developing threats or violence. On the other hand, a refusal might be perceived as insulting. In these cases of violence, the sexual motive changes into a reaction to the sting of wounded pride.

We also grouped 21 incidents beginning with sexual attacks and 15 that began with extreme threats. Following these expressions of force, six targets submitted to sexual assault, because of the level of force exerted. Many immediately began to fight with their assailants. Officers then appeared and the incidents ended short of sexual penetration. Completed rapes depended more on the presence or absence of security than on any type of target response. Most incidents that began with immediate threats moved directly into physical violence. In four cases, violence occurred because aggressors used force when their threats were met with target attempts to withdraw peacefully. In nine cases, targets initiated the violence by responding to the threats with physical force. This set of incidents exemplifies both patterns of sequences resulting in physical violence. Aggressors escalate from threats to physical force, and targets escalate from being the objects of threats to being the initiators of physical violence.

In conclusion, the results of diagraming 150 incidents of sexual aggression may be stated simply. Attacks and threats are often answered by physical violence or threats. Targets tend to answer propositions with threats and aggressors tend to threaten or employ force when propositions have been declined. Thus, dialogue escalates to threats and threats escalate to violence. We could expect little less when violent men enter such transactions.

FEAR, ANGER, AND VIOLENCE

We coded the psychological impact of sexual aggression, tabulating the incidence of specific emotions in each interview. The results of this laborious process showed *fear* and *anger* to be the feelings most often associated with the experience. These are concomitants of violent behavior in both animal and human interactions.

We will first examine the contribution of anger to target violence.

By our definition, targets are recipients of unwanted sexual approaches. Because these approaches are unwanted—obnoxious and offensive—they cause frustration. Targets must often suffer frustration for long periods of time, while aggressors, who play the prison "pimp" role, take pride in their persistence. Because sexual problems are often unshareable problems, men do not talk about them, and they are sometimes afraid to vent their true feelings to aggressors. Frustration, having no release, dams up until it breaks in a flood of aggression. A prisoner tells us:

ARE-4: And when he sat down, he had a cup of coffee in his left hand and he put his right arm around my whole shoulders . . . . And I got so irritated. Nothing would stop him, nothing. Neither threats nor making just sense, or trying to show him my point of view in the situation. Nothing. Nothing would deter it. So he sat down and put his arm around my shoulders and I realized that this was it. I had come to the end of my rope and put up with this crap for long enough. It all happened so fast. I had just come to the end of my rope. And when I jumped up he stood up immediately. I poked at him with that fork, and he backed up because he really thought that I was going to stab him. I was so angry, but I really wasn't going to stab him. I just wanted to make him realize that I could become violent. And like I said, "Back up and if you ever touch me I'll kill you." And I was just ready to enact it. I was at the end. All this pressure just came out at one time.

Aggressors often select targets who seem to have emotional problems that make them more vulnerable. This strategy backfires where targets have difficulty managing aggressivity and hostile feelings. Such men may be locked up because temper control is one of the components of their criminal behavior.

C2-29: The guys were fooling around and grabbing me by the ass. He said I was a pussy and he is going to break me. So I picked him up and I threw him against the wall. When he come off the wall I just beat the pulp out of him. I kind of just lost my head and I know that if I get in that state I am really going to break because, you know, after a while it builds up. You can't take it no longer.

*   *   *

AR-16: He will make a false move and that is when my whole body starts shaking. Like I have got a bad temper and I don't take no shit from nobody. I was close enough to kill one of these dudes around here. I am all nervous and anything could happen.

Of course, confinement can make any prisoner, regardless of his personality, unduly sensitive to irritations. Sexual approaches may impinge on a man already troubled by family worries, resentments over authority, or any of the other possible difficulties of confinement. Sexual pressure in some cases caps a sediment of accumulated aggravations. The target who killed his aggressor tells us:

B-6: At that certain time, I had a whole lot on my mind. He caught me at the wrong time to talk to me about that stuff. If it was another time, I don't believe that I would have tried to kill him or would have tried to do anything to him. I had a whole lot of little things on my mind. It was the time. When I finished, I felt sorry for him. I really shouldn't have done that, but I did it.

RATIONALES FOR VIOLENCE

While some target violence relates to unscheduled explosions of rage, in other cases prisoners say they fight aggressors to carry out calculated aims. Violence, men tell us, becomes the medium for a message and a cool strategy for self-defense.

Defining Sexual Identity

Some targets say they become violent to show others they are straight and mean to stay that way. Most targets dread the gay label. When approached for sex, some avail themselves of the opportunity to attack aggressors so they can publicly demonstrate their disdain of homosexuality. While part of targets' fear revolves around anxiety about being stigmatized, men also feel that if others believe they are gay they will be open to further victimization. This fear relates to the tendency for prisoners to think of targets as "sissies" or "squeeze."

C2-30: It was mostly the same guy and I had to take it out on him because it was getting to a point, you know, everybody in the institution was thinking I was a punk or squeeze or a pussy and stuff like that. I had to do something about it in order to stop it. I had to prove to these other people that I wasn't a pussy or punk or anything else. I had to prove to these other people in my way and their way that I wasn't what he thought I was.

* * *

C2-29: And people was thinking, the people that was looking on at that time, that this guy—well, maybe this guy is a pussy or something. This guy is fooling around with his ass. There must be something wrong with him. He must be a pussy.

So I turned around and I caught him fooling around. So I told him, "Do it once more and I am going to bust you in the face." The people, that is the worst thing in this place, the people look on and they always have their ratings. And they have to gossip. They are like ladies and they really build it up and it runs around the institution.

* * *

CR-28: The guy right next to me, they grab his ass. He just lets it go by and so they call him a squeeze. I told him, "The next time that they touch your ass, you turn around and swing, or otherwise they are going to think that you are a squeeze."

Showing You Believe in the Convict Code

Those identifying with the convict code feel they must answer threat with threat. Such men cannot discuss the problem with the staff, for that shows they are rats. Similarly, the subcultural inmate sometimes cannot reason with an aggressor because he sees talk as a sign of weakness, uncoolness, or as an unacceptable attribute of straight society. Self-respect for prisoners upholding the convict code means favoring private solutions. The correct course of action calls for facing the challenge and responding to it forcefully.

AUI-2: See, when a guy first comes in a lot of guys will say, "Well, I don't want to hit the guy because I am thinking about the parole board." But, really, that is the very best way to deal with it. You could report the incident but that is snitching and I feel myself that if you have to knock the guy's head off to handle the problem, knock the guy's head off. You have to establish yourself as a man and you have to live with yourself. You have to look at yourself every morning in the mirror.

* * *

I: Did you think of any other ways to solve this problem?

AR-41: No, not really. Because what he said was already out in the open. If I talked to him, then everybody else would say I'm trying to cop out. So the only way I seen to solve the problem was to actually get out and fight, prove to him that I ain't going to go to no police and inform on anybody.

Showing You Are Tough

Targets sometimes assert that they are violent because they wish to show others they are tough. Fighting is a way of communicating to all other potential aggressors—not just the men in the immediate incident–that one is not to messed with. Discouraging the immediate approach becomes secondary to raising one's status. The assumption is that a violent demeanor is necessary for survival in prison, and that an aggressive image is a positive and worthwhile attribute of one's public personality, which must be consciously cultivated.

ARE-2: Now, if you were to go out and hit somebody across the head with a pipe and almost kill them, then people would think twice again. They would say, "That dude is crazy and he might try to kill me if I ask him that." And, so, then you know you can go where you want to go.

* * *

C2-23: Now, each and every inmate goes through a trial period here where someone is going to say, "I want your ass." But if he straightens it out himself and he gets into a fight with the guy, it will show everyone that he is not going to take that kind of shit. He will be all right.

* * *

AR-41: I felt kind of different because, like, when I walked through the yard there was people in it that went to school also and they were telling their friends, "This little guy will cut you if you even attempt to do anything to him. He's a dude to stay away from." And you see people looking at you as you're walking by, like saying, "Should I approach him, will he cut me too?" Stuff like this going through their minds.

* * *

C2-27: I wanted to protect myself and the only way that you can protect yourself is with violence. And it was getting to the point where after a while I was starting to do pushups every night. And then as I would get tired, I said that I would kick that guy's ass as I got stronger. I noticed that there was a bunch of them around, I thought when he hit me, "This is it, that will show the other guys when I get into a fight with this one that I'm not going to quit." So I fight and get punched a few times and I punch him a few times and they see that I'm a man.

Violence as a Means of Curbing Violence

Violence can be a simple matter of using preemptive self-defense. At a certain point the target begins to believe that the aggressor is on a course escalating toward a forceful attempt at sexual assault. He then fights to alter this self-conceived prediction. Even men who are approached with nonviolent propositions may project into the future, see themselves as probably victims, and react violently.

C2-43: I was going to grab a bench or a piece of pipe or something and I figured if I hit one of them and they got to bleeding or something they might stop monkeying around.

* * *

A-1: A lot of times fear will make you do things like that. The first time that somebody gives you some lip, you stab him. It's a warning: "Look, I don't want to be pushed around." If somebody comes to you, they can say a word wrong and if you don't react to that one word in the right way, you lose something and then they will test you a little further. If you fail then you're in trouble.

Documenting Violence Effectiveness

Violence as a pragmatic solution is a formula upheld by most inmates. But how does this theory work in actual practice? Is violence, in fact, a successful way to meet the violence problem? On one level, the answer is "yes." In concrete incidents, some men have found violence to be a satisfactory ploy. Targets can report violent responses that have curbed aggressive approaches, and some men who try reasoning with aggressors find them unresponsive until these targets project a more aggressive stance. The effectiveness of protective aggression in certain cases strengthens the norms supporting violence as a solution to forceful sexual approaches.

AR-1: I stood my ground right then and there and I said, "Look, you just stay clear or else I am going to put a pipe right across your head." And I wasn't fooling. And that is the last time he has ever bothered me.

* * *

AR-41: The Spanish dude, after I cut him, he comes back and he says, "Listen, I'm sorry for what I did."
I said, "Do you really mean that? Then I'm sorry for cutting you." I had to put it straight right then, "I'll do it again if you try it again."
And he says, "No, no, everything's all right."

* * *

C2-23: He hit me and then I went after this guy, I beat him—I beat him real good. So about a week later he came back downstairs and all of a sudden he shook my hand and said, "Let's be friends." The only way to get respect from them is to put a foot in their ass.

* * *

AR-7: He went to the hospital and I got locked up. I got a two-day keep-lock even though the administration knew basically that he was behind it. And after that, we more or less became friends, I suppose. We were talking to each other.

* * *

ARE-2: A dude pushed a guy and cut him with a knife. And ever since then people don't do nothing. They talk about it among themselves but whenever he's around, people want to be friends with him.

Negotiating from Weakness

At the same time forces pull men toward violent solutions, other drives push them away from resolving the conflict by verbal negotiation. Especially for those on the brink of feeling powerless, the willingness to negotiate may be seen as an additional symbol of weakness, a further step toward vulnerability. Targets also feel that verbal sparring with aggressors can sink them into deeper trouble than they are in already. Lacking confidence in their bargaining ability, some targets fear that fast-talking "players" will easily manipulate any conversation to serve their ends.

C2-29: You talk to the guy and he bullshits his way out and says this and that and tries to twist your words and throws them back to you. And it doesn't work. He doesn't listen. And the only way he is going to listen at this point is to punch him in the mouth. You can't do anything else.

* * *

A-1: I think they can talk themselves into it deeper. I think that you can talk yourself out of it if you're very slick and if you're mean and have a mean rap. If you have the right eyes, and the right look in your eyes, and the right way of how anger should appear in your eyes, and how hate should appear, and malice, and how to project fear into somebody else's eyes, if you can do that, you can do it, you can talk your way out of it. But the thing is that if you're too scared, then you loose.

* * *

C2-23: You try to talk to them—you try to talk sense to them and say, "Now, look, I am an inmate and you are an inmate."
And they will say, "Ah—don't tell me that pussy shit." They will tell you that, you know. So, I figured that talking was no good with this guy. There is only one way to handle him and that is to fight with him.

* * *

A-1: I hadn't even tried to talk them out of it, because I wasn't that good at expressing myself and I couldn't project fear into someone. I couldn't project hositility. There was something that I couldn't do.

PEER AND STAFF SUPPORT

The attitudes and behaviors associated with target violence are in part social behavior, learned in prison from other inmates and staff. Targets are generally new to the prison where they are harassed by sexual aggression; they may look to others for guidance. Peers, often men who have been targets themselves, may advise new men to consider violence favorably. Men who have never used weapons are supplied with "shanks" and "pipes" by their more experienced friends. Others are supplied with arguments through which guilt is neutralized. The target's violent response is an explicit normative expectation of the prison community. This is passed on to new men by experienced inmates as part of the process of "prisonization."

AR-23: And I went out in the yard and I told my brother what was happening. The next thing you know one of my brother's friends came up and gave me a shank and told me that if a guy come up at me to stick him.

* * *

C2-52: He just told me to grab anything that I can and just beat them. Whether it is a chair or whatever and just go after them.

* * *

C2-22: This black dude was going to jump a friend of mine and so I talked to him and I said, "Look, man, the knife drawer is open. Grab one of them butcher knives and bring it upstairs. That is all." He took the knife out of the drawer and put it in the back of his pants and went upstairs and stuck it in the pillow and sewed the pillow back up. And if this dude come over, he would have got stabbed.

* * *

C2-28: I just said, "Look-it, you just pick up something and you hit that dude. Or else you go and you make yourself a blade and you stab the dude—do anything." I says, "If the dude is going to rip you off, you kill the dude—that is all."

* * *

AR-36: He was the water man and he was pretty straight. He came right out and he told me, "You are a little guy and you can expect trouble, you know, but if anything happens, don't even question it, just crack their skull and it will be over with—that is all."

* * *

C2-30: I go over and pull him over in the corner and talk to him right then and there and tell him, "These guys are trying to get over on you. The best thing for you to do is to hang out with the white guys and try and get to know people. Lift weights. Try boxing and do what you can. Learn how to fight if you can't fight."

* * *

C2-23: I told him that the best thing to do, in front of everyone, while this guy was popping shit to him, is to hit the guy.

There is no other way that this thing is going to be resolved unless you hit the guy.

* * *

C2-44: I don't know how many times I told him, "If a dude run up on you, popping you some shit, just hit him in his face. If you lose, you lose—so what? You get locked up for seven days and you come downstairs and the dude will think twice before running up on you again. Because they are going to know that you will hurt him."

* * *

AR-6: So I tried to talk about it with some of the white guys that was here. They was living on this tier with me. And they tried to give me solutions. The majority of them told me to hit this guy, anybody that come up to you, just hit him.

The advocacy of violence is spread by the old to the young and by the experienced to the inexperienced. Thus, in observing how targets are readied to behave violently, we see a process whereby a subculture upholding violence spreads its message. Moreover, the learning that occurs in these peer groups is not academic. It answers an immediate problem of pressing concern to the learner.

Staff

Staff members also support target violence so that the square or isolate inmate who identifies with officialdom can learn violent norms just as well as the group member who identifies with his peers. Why do staff uphold violent solutions? Some staff members have cultural origins similar to those of many inmates in the prison. They are working-class men themselves and hold norms supporting "masculine" responses to intimidation. In addition, staff, like inmates, belong to the prison community. This community, as a norm of its own, holds that a violent response is one of the simplest and most effective ways of handling an aggressive sexual approach. Finally, staff, especially officers, sometimes can think of no options that they know to work as well as a violent response.

C2-20: And the C.O. came in and asked what had happened and I told him that this guy had tried to take me off and I was just protecting myself. So then the C.O. said, "I'll shut the door and you do what you think is the best." And so I fucked the guy up and sent him to the hospital.

* * *

AR-46: In Attica, they told me to take a pipe to them if they bother you sexually. Take a pipe to them them—that was the officers. I was told that in '65 and so I started using one.

* * *

C2-51: The officer with me in the hall—he said, "You should have hit him in the nuts." And I said, "I am not a dirty fighter." He said, "That don't make no difference, man, you just do that." And I guess after a while I found out that he was right. So after a while, after I took it under deep study, I had the trouble and I hit him in the nuts.

* * *

AR-36: He [lieutenant] said, being a little guy, if anything like that should happen, hit the guy with the first thing available and try and knock him down. Try and do it in front of a hack or somebody and then he will come down and break it up. Once they do, you will go to the box. And once you get to the box, tell the hacks that you want to see me. I will come up, see what I can do. That is about the only thing that I can tell you.

* * *

I: So you spoke to the priest about this sex pressure, too? Did he offer you any advice?

* * *

C2-52: He just told me to do what I think is best and just fight if I have to.

* * *

I: You went to your company officer?

C2-23: Right. I went and said, "Look, this guy is bothering me, man. He keeps coming out with these sexual remarks and I want somebody to do something about this guy—tell him something." He said, "Well, there is nothing that we can do about it, and there is nothing that the brass can do about it, so hit him." He came right out and told me just like that.

During informal conversations, as when an officer on his rounds pauses to discuss an inmate's problem with him, the staff advise targets to be violent. Staff also offer this advice as part of the formal delivery of counseling services. Administrators, counselors, and even chaplains participate in giving such advice. The message that is communicated through official channels is essentially the same message as the men receive from their peers. Its content mirrors the themes we have reviewed: Violence will win you respect; it will deter future approaches; it will cause the aggressor bothing you to back off. Prison records show staff pleased with such advice, convinced of its effectiveness. When one inmate applied for transfer, his counselor wrote:

> Because of his youthful appearance, other inmates saw him as a prime material for homosexual activities. Through counseling and an individually tailored body building program, John has developed self-confidence and asserted his individuality. Having made his adjustment here, he should be able to hold his own in a camp setting.

When prisoners fight, they face staff discipline. Formal procedures can remove privileges and sentence men to solitary confinement. In some cases of sexual aggression, however, informal arrangements suspend disciplinary proceedings, enabling staff to back up their advice with supportive leniency. When staff view inmate violence as justified and practical, formal measures to stop violence may be suspended: Staff may make private arrangements to overlook a fight provided it is in the service of survival. Staff thus monitor and even encourage instrumental inmate assaults on other inmates.

C2-37: I said, "Well, there is a nigger wanted to make me a kid." I says, "Before I give my ass up to any nigger, I would fucking kill him." So he [staff] says, "Well, you have got a point there." He says, "Yeah, all right, I am going to let you go." I said, "Any keep-lock or anything?" And he says, "You have got one day keep-lock and the next time any nigger or anything comes up on you, you do the same thing."

* * *

C2-31: One sergeant told me, "Put a bat across this dude's head and I will go to court and testify that you told me about this shit."

* * *

AR-36: When I went through my orientation, the senior lieutenant told me that if anything like that should happen, "Hit him, and when you go to the box, send the word and I will come up and talk to you. I will do what I can to get you out of trouble."

* * *

C2-30: I asked Sergent Brown. And he told me to go ahead, "Pick up the nearest thing around you and hit him in the head with it. He won't bother you no more." I went over to another sergeant and I asked him and he said, "Pick up the nearest damn thing to you and just hit him with it, that is all." I looked at him and I said, "All right. If I do this I ain't going to get locked up for it, am I?" He looks at me and he says, "No." Because I am using self-defense.

PROBLEMS WITH VIOLENT SOLUTIONS

The violent response to sexual approaches may be effective for some, but not for others. As Bartollas et al. (1976) point out, such values, in institutions, are "functional for aggressive inmates . . . the code clearly works to the disadvantage of the weak" (p. 69). Such men take into prison ideas opposed to violence while others have limited experience with violence. Men also have types of personality that make violent behavior a difficult—or impossible—solution for them. According to Toch (1977), norms that prescribe violence create a difficult situation for inmates to whom violence is "ego alien."

A 7: The minute I think about what to do to a guy and how they butcher them and this and that, all that runs through my mind is blood. That scares the hell out of me. I don't like this. I wouldn't want to cut up anybody just like I wouldn't want them to cut me up. . . . I am not a fighter, man, that's not my bag and I won't do it. I hardly did any fighting out on the streets. And they just told me to take a guy, take a club, and club him. And I never did that to a guy.

* * *

APC-14: If you are an aggressive person, like a bigmouth, you stand a chance of people steering away from you. But if you're reserved, they'll run all over you. But I'm quiet and I don't think that I have got to adjust to them people. In other words, if I have got to be getting up and saying, "Hey, motherfucker," and make up lies that I did this and that, just to keep them away from me, then I could do it. But it's not my thing.

* * *

APCC-4: It wasn't easy because I felt that he would see through me. Because I'm not that way naturally. And I thought that he would see through me and laugh at me.

While some violent reactions to sexual approaches are informally tolerated by officials, fear of institutional discipline restrains many men. They want to avoid punishment, losing good time, or being sentenced anew. Such repercussions are particularly likely when the target exceeds the limits of violence tolerated by authorities. For example, the man who murdered the aggressor who propositioned him received a sentence of five years. Another target sliced a man across the face, giving him a wound requiring 22 stitches, and he received a sentence of 22 years. This man also received a wide range of punishments available to the prison administration. He tells us:

AR-35: They took me to special housing unit called the guard house and they put me in a stripped cell. No bed. No nothing. Just a toilet bowl and a sink. They left me there 38 days—just feeding me—took all my clothes and everything. I didn't have anything except for a toilet bowl and a sink and after a while I had an inmate sneak me a blanket and when the officers come by I would have to sneak it back to him. Then they took me to court and prosecuted me—assault in the first degree. They gave me 22 years. Before I went to trial, I was placed in a security cell for 38 days and taken to the superintendent's hearing and was prosecuted. And I had been punished about four or five times for that crime.

The fear of disciplinary infractions or of few charges puts some targets in a dilemma. Should they consider their long-term welfare or fight to alleviate an aggressor's pressure? Peer and staff support may facilitate personal aggression but cannot grant immunity to consequences. This means that the fear of punishment may outweight the perceived benefits of violence.

Fear of punishment complicates the problem "solved" by the norm of violence. Similarly, the norms are no "solution" for those unable to fight because they are unprepared, socially and psychologically, to meet tough urban sexual aggressors. These men are in especially difficult positions. Unable to avail themselves of the escape provided by the convict culture, they are plagued by feelings of inadequacy. Knowing that violence is the "correct" course of action but not being able to implement it, they are failures in the convict world. The normative advice cannot help them, and they must seek other, perhaps less attractive, solutions to the problem. These are the men who often go to the solitary confinement of protective custody—"protection companies"—men who may live in fear throughout their stay in prison (Lockwood, 1977a).

CONCLUSION

About half of 152 incidents of sexual aggression I examined involved physical violence. Half of this violence came from aggressors who attempted to coerce targets; the rest came from targets who reacted to threats or perceived threats. Violent reactions are instrumental for targets in the sense that they end more incidents than any other reactions. After fights, targets tell us, aggressors leave them alone. They move around the prison with less fear and feel better about themselves.

Most men we interviewed had attitudes and values supporting violent solutions to the problem of being a target. Prisoners see violence as the medium for the message that one is straight, uninterested in sexual involvement, or that one is tough, not a prospect to "get over on." Others say that violence is the best self-defense available. Reacting with force unambiguously lets the aggressor know the consequences of his behavior if he persists. In prison, target violence usually leads to an improved self-image and a more favorable status among other prisoners. Fellow inmates, looked to for guidance, school new inmates to accept this solution. Staff support target violence and back up their counsel with a flexible disciplinary process, exempting some inmates from punishment when they fight to uphold their manhood.

Other psychological factors complement these ideas supporting inmate violence. Anger characterizes the target emotional response. The irritation caused by aggressors can itself lead to targets exploding in unpredictable and uncalculated ways. As in ethology, fear and anger are linked to aggression. Threatened men, angered men, become aggressive and turn aggressors into victims.

The Impact of Victimization

 The behavior discussed in this book is defined as aggressive because it produces some degree of psychologically tangible harm. Part of my research task was to locate, record, quantify, and analyze this harm. Over 100 in-depth interviews, tape-recorded and transcribed, form the factual basis for reporting the effects of sexual victimization on male prisoners. In the Chapters 4 and 5, I trace the impact of aggressive episodes on targets' emotions, attitudes, and lifestyles and explore the reasons for such impacts. I show how problems that derive from target experiences relate to other personal problems men face in prison. As the second of these chapters is devoted exclusively to the impact of prison rape on its victims, the interview excerpts in the first of these chapters are provided by prisoners who have not been rape victims but who have been sexually attacked or sexually threatened, or who see themselves as targets of aggression after being propositioned.

Using the research technique of content analysis, responses were first categorized and then counted from the lengthy interview transcriptions. Although this method was laborious, it had distinct advantages. At the time of the interview, I could concentrate on encouraging my informants to share thoughts and feelings they had at the time of the interview freely. Thus, I could devote my full attention to listening, giving appropriate feedback, and asking probing questions that motivated informants to talk about themes in the depths of their minds—themes often crucially important to them, yet topics about which many had seldom talked before. Research data like this cannot be accumulated with systematic research instruments such as questionnaires. Yet, in order to capture and describe the range of personal reactions to victimization accurately, a precise, empirical method was necessary. Content analysis, where varieties of reaction are categorized and counted after the open-ended interviews take place, combines the precision of the survey with the psychological depth of the counseling interview. It proved to be an excellent method for the study of prison sexual aggression.

EMOTIONAL REACTIONS

Fear

In 55 percent of the incidents they described, targets told me they experienced fear. This was the most common emotion reported. Regardless of the level of force they met, many targets, following incidents, believed themselves to be future candidates for prison rape. Thus, the fear they felt often took the form of apprehension that they might shortly become victims of actual sexual assault. Frequently, long after incidents initially inspiring fear are over, men continue to view themselves as open to imminent attack. Since such fear is so subjectively inspired, men can cultivate such feelings without concrete events. The worry that one may be raped can, and does, thrive in dangerous settings, without much direct personal experience with sex aggression. Targets, however, knowing other men are attracted to them, are more susceptible than others to such fear:

AC-10: I think it was just the fear that this type of aggression could happen. That here I had done nothing to this guy, had never even spoken to him, and I'd been selected from all this group of 35 guys, that I had been singled out of all these.

* * *

C2-23: Nobody likes the idea of somebody ripping his pants off with the help of other people helping him and sticking his dick in his ass. Nobody likes that idea, even the thought of it. You figure your pride, your own self-pride, your own ego, humiliation, the pain, whatever. A whole lot of things start to get you and you are not going to let this person do this to you. Use you like you are some kind of animal. And this builds up to a certain point and then it is a breaking point.

Men who conceive fear based on an incident can go on to generalize this apprehension so that it colors their perception of the entire prison environment. They may see danger everywhere; they may believe that encounters with other men are likely to disintegrate into aggressive episodes; and since prison is packed with men, they may see potential terrors in every part of their prison world:

ARE-7: A group of guys would be kidding each other about your hind end. Eventually I realized that they were kidding, but I was taking it serious. I just evaded them and I started being alone and staying by myself. I was never approached but I was always scared. I always had it on my mind. I would watch all the corners. I was really shook at the time they moved me to D Block because I was scared of that and I guess I was scared of the general population.

* * *

C2-53: I may be over that point of having to prove myself, but I still watch myself from an aggressiveness from anybody. I guess you can say that I am on the paranoid side.

* * *

APCC-4: I just watched myself when I was out in the yard. I would watch everything that was going on. I guess I was just more aware. I was just becoming more aware of my surroundings and where I was.

Fear persists when targets and aggressors live together in close proximity after incidents. Residual feelings make targets believe they have made permanent enemies. Then they may view contact with aggressors as a sign of weakness, a signal inviting more sexual overtures. This blocks any chance for reconciliation. Speaking only to those in their trusted cliques, fear grows on uncertain cues. Misunderstandings are magnified:

ARE-4: You walk out into the yard and you walk in the mess hall and it is not just a feeling because you will turn around and you will look and this guy will be staring right at you. And you will stare back at him for a second and then turn away and then you look back and he is still staring. And it upsets me. It really does. You don't know then what the guy is thinking. The first thing that runs through your mind is, "Oh, my God, he is looking at me for sexual activity or something like this." And the only way you can describe it is frightening.

* * *

AR-36: Whenever I see him around I am consciously aware of it. No matter what I am doing I have to keep in the back of my mind where he is. Not that he would try anything out there in the yard or anything, but the thing is, you never know. He might be a bug. He actually was gone for three months. They had him down to Matteawan and now he is back. I don't know if he might just flip out some day. I will just cross the yard and then he'll come running around, across the yard, and go crazy. I have always got it in my mind whenever he is around to be well aware.

* * *

C2-27: When you're in the showers in Elmira, then sometimes there is 20 or 30 people in the shower, and they're always making remarks to you. You don't feel free. I'm used to being on the streets where you don't have any paranoia. Taking a shower is a beautiful thing. Here it's a paranoia thing where they have your back against the wall. And if you turn around and wash your legs and you've bent over, besides getting remarks, you might get really hurt. I still keep my back to the shower, and I wash my back and watch everything. It's a weird thing, that if you drop something you don't even bend down to pick it up. You say, fuck it, I lost a bar of soap. I'm just not going to bend over and get whistles and feel really stupid. And you just pull your pants down and there is all these guys just waiting for you to pull your pants down. It's a sick thing. Even though the physical pressure is there for a short time, the mental pressure is there permanently. And if you're on the toilet and everybody is just walking by, then it's really an intense thing. I've been to the bathroom in front of people on the streets and it's just nothing at all like it is in here. You just want to say, "Jesus, leave me alone." But you can't close the door. It's a cell and people are looking in at you. You feel kind of helpless.

Anger

Next to fear, anger is the most common emotion we find, with 42 percent of the targets reporting this feeling. I discuss more fully the implications of this anger in Chapter 3 ("Target Violence"). At this time, however, let us emphasize the similarity of this emotional response in prison to females facing sexual aggression in free society. A study provides data on this question: Women, objects of aggressive approaches (mostly falling short of rape), reported their feelings in questionnaires given by Kanin and Kirkpatrick (1953). While guilt, fear, and disgust were widely mentioned, anger was the emotion most often reported in this survey. In part because of the prevalence of anger in such incidents, sexual aggressors often become victims of their targets. The object of sexual force then suffers twofold. The harm caused by the sexual aggressor is compounded by the legal trouble the target is in when his or her anger precipitates violence.

Anger can directly cause significant harm. When social interaction results in one party becoming angry at another party, communication falters. Mutual misunderstanding grows. Potential for violence increases dramatically. In the case of sexual aggression, the angry target often insults the aggressor, who then becomes angry himself. Incidents beginning with low levels of aggression (for example, verbal propositions for sexual involvement) can escalate into highly charged violent encounters. Targets who do not become involved in this violence can also suffer when anger, surviving in unexpressed form, leads to frustration and tension. Incidents that cause anger are thus victimizing incidents. Targets can be harmed by participating in violence motivated by their anger or their anger can lead to internal or psychological discomfort. For example:

52: Well, I was doing the pans and they come up to me and they said, "We are going to fuck you in the ass." And I didn't pay no attention to them and they kept on saying it. They just kept on saying that we are going to fuck you in the ass, so I turned around and I said, "Like fuck you are," and I walked over, and I grabbed one of those big spoons that we make the soup with and I went after them and I started swinging at them and they both lost their cool and someone yelled fight and four C.O.s came in and grabbed us and I was locked up for 13 days.

Anxiety

In one-third of the incident descriptions, men clearly describe feeling anxious—defined as uneasiness, apprehension, or tension. Often men told of physiological indicators of stress, reporting shaking, crying, stuttering, weakness, and inability to sleep or concentrate. While anxiety can be present without such indicators, behavioral cues help assess the psychological impact of victimization:

A-8: I don't know where the change was, but I've had numerous people say that I was shaking and scared and trembling. I was nervous.

* * *

C2-27: I got so wired up about it that in Elmira I got ulcers from it. I would be throwing up blood and then, out of frustration, I would eat a lot. I came in weighing 125 pounds and I don't know if it was psychological or not, but I just kept on eating and I got to be 180 pounds.

* * *

AR-6: I couldn't get myself to write a letter or to play my guitar. I couldn't listen to music or concentrate on nothing.

* * *

C2-15: My hands would get all sweated up and everything. When I am talking about it my hands get all sweaty. When I talk about it, I get all tensed up, you know. I go to sleep at night and I would wake up in the morning and I would have cramps and my legs would be crampy and sometimes I would throw up. I have not thrown up in two or three years and here I am throwing up not over something that I ate but how I feel.

* * *

APC-11: Once in awhile I would be sitting there and putting a crossword puzzle together or reading a book and I figured that I was calm. And then, all of a sudden, my hand would start shaking and I couldn't stop it for a while. Once in a while you will get a few pains in your chest and you lay back and you think you are having a heart attack. I mean it feels like you have lost your breath and you jump up quick like that and try to get your breath.

The anxiety targets feel can extend far beyond the duration of the physical incident, and can sometimes last as long as men are imprisoned. During this time, relatively minor encounters with those one perceives to be aggressive set off renewed attacks of nervous tension. Even though a man no longer is a target, he still feels like one, and this feeling can become a dominant preoccupation:

C2-6: Ever since the day that I got in here I thought about it and I will think about it until I get out. All day and during the time at night until I go to sleep. It's just something stuck in my head and I have to do something about it. I've tried and tried to do something about it, but no one ever does anything about it.

*   *   *

C2-20: I didn't sleep at night, I had to get some sleep sometime during the day. I couldn't sleep very well. Here I can hear and see down the hall and up there I couldn't hear anybody coming. But now I can hear and close my eyes and hear if anybody is approaching. And if somebody is approaching me like that, then I would jump out of bed and look around and see who is coming near me.

*   *   *

C2-27: There's so much shit in here all the time and you're so keyed up all the time, that when you finally sleep, you lay down and sleep and sleep and sleep. And it comes on you, every night. Sometimes I've wanted to wake up and just write down some of the wild shit that I've dreamed about. You never feel at ease. The blacks trying to fuck you and the blacks trying to lower you and trying to fuck you. The whole situation. I know that personally I would like to let out a few exhales out and just sort of calm down a bit.

It's gotten so bad that about a month ago I started talking to the shrink. I said, "I'm really feeling a lot of tension." So he's got me on a drug at night and another drug during the day. And I'm in my cell and I'm fine now. I'm a zombie. I walk around really loaded and it's all right.

Some men have nervous conditions when they come to prison. (Again, they may, for this reason, be preferred targets.) Such persons are particularly driven to anxiety when they confront aggressors. They feel stress more sharply than others, and their breakdown point is often nearer. With others, anxiety is "situational," related only to special circumstances, not particular mental states. In both cases, severe stress can result in crisis, our next topic.

Crisis

Hans Toch (1975) explores motives for self-mutilation among prisoners. Toch and his associates, Fox (1976), Johnson (1976), and Gibbs (1978), interviewed over 400 New York State prisoners who injured themselves. Most of these men attempted suicide by hanging or by cutting their wrists with razor blades or broken pieces of glass. Toch's subject, however, is "breakdown," not just its physical indicators. Breakdown follows severe disruption. It results in stress, a "set of reactions that make it impossible for the person to continue functioning as he would ordinarily" (Toch, 1975, p. 2). Specifically, breakdown in prison can lead to men isolating themselves, or becoming "disoriented, paralyzed, or helplessly self-destructive" (Toch, 1975, p. 70).

Fear is an element in breakdown, according to Toch, when an individual sees himself inescapably as vulnerable. "Self-doubt," Toch (1975) states, "translates into fear when a man thinks that the odds against him are overwhelming" (p. 68). The subject's thoughts and feelings contribute to his condition. In extreme cases, in fact, no independently definable stimulus is necessary for a total collapse from fear. We must look to how danger is perceived in order to comprehend victim experiences. Self-doubt itself can explain some stress reactions. When one sees oneself as weak, as ineffective or inadequate, it is easy to envision oneself as a potential victim. The fear this inspires can be more damaging to a prisoner than the objective danger an outsider would see. This entails a dilemma for security forces because physical custody alone fails to solve the problem.

What happens when men break down from fear? Some feelings—hopelessness, and confusion, for example lead to self-imposed isolation or self-injury when men become disoriented or paralyzed. Feelings of frustration may lead to violent acts for which men are punished by officials or harmed by the inmates to whom they react. However, if rage is repressed, it can lead to tension. Fearful behavior by victims can also encourage aggressors. When men show self-doubt in their demeanor, they attract aggressors searching for the weak. Fear, translated into doubt about how one will handle future encounters, can actually precipitate such encounters. When this occurs, when the prophecy is fulfilled, the mental effect can be doubly devastating.

According to Toch (1975), a man in crisis "conveys the message that he is not surviving with integrity in his situation" (p. 322). Burgess and Holmstrom (1974) define crisis as "a disequilibrium to an individual's life style" (p. 300). A person "in crisis" is frequently made visible through change in his behavior. When prisoners face severe problems that they are failing to solve satisfactorily, their inner turmoil can show up in appeals for help, self isolation, and suicidal thoughts or gestures.

Relying on the above definitions, we coded 24 percent of the sexual targets as being in crisis following incidents. (Keep in mind, however, that our staff referrals and our protection interviews make this figure unrepresentative since we sampled from unique groups that were more likely than others to have suffered extreme effects from sex aggression.) Many men classified themselves in the crisis group by speaking of "bugging out," "flipping out," "not being able to take it," or "having a nervous breakdown." Here are other examples:

C2-14: Well, sometimes when I am in my cell, I feel that this problem is coming. I try to avoid it and I feel like I want to jump up and just break everything—everything in my cell but I try to keep my head and calm myself down or do something. Really, I feel like trying to do something—break a wall or something.

* * *

AC-10: I was really an emergency case the second day that I was here. I had so many fears and so many worries going in my head. I felt really such a broken spirit. I guess you might say that all I could do was crawl under the concrete.

* * *

A7: I was all torn up inside with nerves. I was sick, sick, sick, constantly, right straight through for two weeks. I didn't want to be put out in the population. I wanted to be put someplace where I could work with no one around me. Then I would be fine, but I know that you can't do this. There is no such thing like that in here.

Men in crisis may see themselves approaching mental illness. Sensing themselves as going under, they look for help. Their condition, thus, can be signaled by requests for therapeutic assistance, or for emergency transfer out of the stress inducing environment:

ARC-14: I said I wanted to go to protection and he said, "No, I'm not going to put you in protection, not until something happens." And then the next day or something he came around me. And then I got very emotionally upset. Then he said they would put me in protection.

* * *

C2-45: He said, "I am going to cut you up." And so the guard came and I told the guard that I just can't stand it no more, "put me in keep-lock or something. Get me the hell out of here. I can't stand this environment."

Crises are often serious problems that we can neither solve nor escape. When requests for aid get nowhere, when one's personal stock of solutions is depleted, one is left with an unsolvable problem. At this point, some men declare bankruptcy; their fear of sexual aggression leads to thoughts of suicide:

CR-26: I was just so confused and everything. Because of that, I just didn't care anymore and I felt to myself if they are going to rip me off for my ass, I am going to cut up and go over to the hospital and they can't get me over there. I just didn't care. I had been put away most of my life and half of my life was ruined anyways, so why should I live with the pain and heartbreaks ever since I was 9 years old, and I was to the point where I didn't care anymore.

There are more suicide attempts recorded in prison institutional files for both aggressors and targets than for nontargets. In part, this difference reflects the fact that aggressors and targets are younger than nontargets, for youths in prison are in a high risk group for suicide attempts (Toch, 1975). Targets, however, are more than twice as likely than agressors and more than 17 times as likely as nontargets to have made attempts on their own lives: 38 percent of all targets have made a suicidal gesture in prison.

Although some recorded acts of self-mutilation are undoubtedly tied to specific target incidents, data in institutional files are not detailed enough for us to make this connection. A suicide attempt may be associated with having been a target since both situations are linked to fear. Toch (1975) indicates one category of difficulty some targets experience, which he calls "fate avoidance." It indicates a feeling of powerlessness to cope with a fearful situation—a helplessness to avoid or protect oneself from harm. A person with such a problem makes a suicidal attempt because he wishes to avoid being harmed and sees being harmed as an unavoidable fate. Targets from protective environments are almost twice as likely as randomly selected targets to attempt suicide. Again, just as accelerated feelings of fear drive men to protection, they drive men to take their lives. Men are made fearful by target incidents: Target incidents confirm the worst expectations of already fearful men; fearful men are also more likely to be inviting targets.

When targets in crisis think about cutting their wrists or hanging themselves, they are generally assuming that the aggressor will get to them no matter what they do. As we have seen, one encounter with an aggressor is sometimes enough to let one believe that his fate as a victim is sealed. When this type of fear becomes combined with feelings of powerlessness, with a sense that one cannot escape what he sees as his fate, the problem becomes insoluble:

A-7: Death. That's all I could think of. I had this fear in me and I thought that one of these days I was going to be surprised and I didn't know who was going to do it. So that is why the fear got in me and went deeper and deeper and deeper and then it got so that I would shake and shake. And when it got to that, then I was really scared. This [suicide] did occur to me. I said they would never bring me back here alive. I said that I would never come back here again. I'm not adapted to doing a bit at all. And I could never do time. I never want to do time again. I would beg for the electric chair if I had to do time. I wouldn't want to stay here. I can't do time. I can't walk out there without worrying if someone is setting me up.

                              *   *   *

C2-18: I was thinking about cutting my wrists and then I was trying—thinking about trying to hang myself. I figured that when I was locked out that sooner or later the blacks would get me. If I stayed up in that division they would get me one way or the other.

                              *   *   *

C2-45: The dude in the shower felt my ass. I figured that I was going to be a goner, and they would take my manhood or something. So I just cut up and then I chickened out. I wanted to kill myself or some stupid shit like this. I said, "Fuck it, man." I went to my cell and I took my mirror and I just slashed through. I didn't cut very deep but the blood was still running and then I said if they send me to Matteawan, then it will be on my record that I bugged out and that I cut up and I said, "Piss on it." And I wiped it off and I went through some pain for about two weeks and then it healed up, without anybody seeing it.

In about 20 percent of the incidents, targets told us that they had thought about suicide. However, only a few men actually reached the point of injuring themselves. Some of these men felt hopeless and just wanted the peace of mind they saw available in death. Others hoped that staff would remove them from the danger they were in. They hoped to be transferred immediately, for example, to the mental hospital maintained for prisoners by the state. Ironically, statements from former inmates suggest this mental hospital may have had one of the highest levels of sexual aggression in the state.

Many targets in crisis deal with their problems through less drastic means than self injury by requesting protective housing (Lockwood, 1977a,b). Even though protection in the adult prison means confinement in a single cell for 22 hours a day, and men in protection are generally stigmatized by others, such sanctuaries offer safety. They allow men a chance to restore psychological equilibrium. Some staff, when they learn of the inmate's problems, help him by transferring him to a different job or living area. Staff frequently made such transfers without letting everyone know what the problem was: Sensitive to men's needs, they attempted to avoid the isolation and stigma that are the corollaries of flight strategies.

Crises combine many of the feelings targets tell us they experience. Fear is the root cause, to which is added anxiety and tension. The pressure builds up when men cannot solve their problem, i.e., when they cannot find a way to feel safe or self-sufficient. Suicidal thoughts and gestures may come as men look for escape. Many crises are resolved with the help of staff or by moving to established protective environments.

IMPACT IN CONTEXT

Most incidents, as we have seen, occur relatively early in men's sentences, at a time when many prisoners also worry about separation from families. Entering prison, men feel great concern for the life they have been forced to leave behind. Especially acute tension arises when men who formerly took care of others are now rendered helpless. Not being able to do anything about problems at home, all prisoners are able to do is worry about them. The entry period can also be a time when guilt and remorse bother men. Legal complexities, always trying, persist. Burdened with problems, new prisoners find confinement no tomb for the living, although they may wish for a tranquil place to mend their wounds. Prison is a tumultuous, stimulus-filled environment, a world whose complexity is greatly heightened by exposure to unfamiliar cultures. Consequently, responses to sexual aggression can become mixed with responses to other difficulties of confinement:

AC-10: People would come up to me and ask me about my crime and what I had done and this is a terrible part of my life and I don't want to talk about it. I had terrible regrets. And then this black guy came in and he was telling me that they would be selling me for 20 cartons a piece . . . and certainly it frightened me. And also having to bear the fear and the anxiety of being in prison and being confronted with an environment that I was totally unfamiliar with. Not knowing what was going to happen and then be surrounded, actually flooded with this kind of conversation.

* * *

ARE-4: I have a wife and two kids and she's living with her mother and no car right now. Every time that my wife comes up to visit me and she goes home again, her mother calls her a half-time mother. She is trying to discourage my wife from coming up and seeing me and she discourages my oldest boy. She is telling him that you don't have a father and things like this. And now this starts to bother me. But when you have to cope with a situation that arises in the institution as far as homosexuality, this puts another burden on top of another burden and there are just so many things that a man can cope with before he breaks. A man does have more problems than he came in with, without adding to them. And then you get into a situation like this and before you can really get into the program and get relaxed— because it is a heck of a shock to come into a place like this—before you get a chance to do this, you've got another problem built up.

* * *

AC-10: I was just so totally saturated with fear. Also being very upset over finding myself in prison, having to even try to figure out how I allowed myself to get into something that I would have let go this far.

I was so overwhelmed with so many fears and so many

problems that I was confronted with, plus trying to adjust to finding yourself locked in a cell so many hours a day, that it was very difficult for me to even try to figure out things, or to try to get any kind of plan as to how I could cope with the future. It was almost a day to day groping, really, of trying to muster through all the fear and anxiety and depression that I had. There did not seem to be any way of having a little extra corner of your mind that you can say, well, this is used for planning and plotting your way through. I was just so overwhelmed by all this.

LIFE-STYLE CHANGES

When a man is a target, the incident can affect the way he lives as much as the way he thinks. As we have seen, targets in crisis often move to new locations in attempts to cope with the problem. Such life-style changes, compelled by sex aggression, can be viewed as "secondary victimization." Most targets (87 percent) reported disruption of their lives following incidents. Men who became violent were disciplined. Nonviolent men stopped going to certain places in order to be more secure. Although targets in crisis may seek the total seclusion of protection, less traumatized men quietly cut off certain activities. They trade a certain amount of freedom for increments in security:

AC-10: I just go to lunch and that is all. And I manage then to do my own thing as far as breakfast and dinner is concerned.

* * *

APC-11: I didn't go out in the yard or nothing. I just stayed in my cell and went to work and went right back and stayed in my cell. I never went out in the yard. I didn't ever even dare to go out in the yard, really.

The most common change in life-style is some degree of self-isolation. It can be formal, as in protection or keep-lock, or informal, as when men stay in their cells whenever the prison routine permits them to do so. Self-imposed isolation is a voluntary response to the threat of victimization. In some cases, it is routinized, and entire classes of target-prone men may consign themselves to degrees of confinement more severe than those under which others live. Such is the case, for example, in some large urban jails where young white prisoners live in protection units.

We interviewed all the men living in formal protective custody status in several prisons, and we saw the role of "segregation" in the management of inmate fear (Lockwood, 1977a,b). About a third of Attica's protection population was there because of sex pressure. These men were more brittle and more traumatized than the targets we interviewed who survived in the general population. Protection men reacted to incidents by opting for 22 hours a day of lockup, totally removed from prison activities. It was a seemingly harsh solution: The men were denied movies, school, church, work. Other prisoners looked down on them for living in "pediatrics," calling them "punks" and "pussies." Because others thought they had willingly engaged in the passive role in homosexual behavior, targets in protection were also called "homos." Because other prisoners thought these men had shared their troubles with staff, they were called "rats." In a gallery that was shut off from the rest of the prison, protection men had to stay locked in their cells for all but a brief part of each day. Nonetheless, in spite of the obvious liabilities of protection, most targets declared themselves satisfied with the arrangement when compared to the dangers they would face in population.

In the youth prison (Coxsackie), C-2 or "Weak Company" was the functional equivalent of protection. Having existed in the youth prison for as long as veteran staff could remember, Weak Company was a systemic response to the need for giving special protection to youths who were bullied by others. At the time of our interviews, Weak Company (90 percent white) held about a quarter of all white prisoners in the youth institution. Most Weak Men, like other whites, had been targets of sexual aggression at one time or another.

The youth prison was run more strictly than the adult prison. Guards marched companies of men to and fro. Prisoners were locked in single cells except at activities, which were always well-controlled. Because life in the youth prison was more structured and because free choice and free movement were limited, targets under pressure had to isolate themselves less often than in the adult prison. In the adult prison, informal self isolation was a more common response to sexual aggression. Like the elderly in New York City's troubled South Bronx, some adult targets only went out at certain times when they felt safe, and then only when it was absolutely necessary. Potential amenities of life were sacrificed for peace of mind. Paradoxically, the prison reform that makes things looser, that gets men out of cells and gives them more freedom of movement, can also result in making prisons more dangerous. It induces, for some types of men, more isolation than they had experienced before reform. Locks and bars and guards protect men from each other as much as they keep men from escaping. As the following examples show, the target experience causes men to stay in the shelter of their cells even though they could leave if they so desired.

AP-10: Well, like, if I ever did come out of my cell I usually stopped at my door and looked this way and that and made sure everything was clear before I even moved. If I had the faintest idea that somebody was watching me, I just closed my door and went back in. Because I didn't take no chances on anything.

* * *

ARE-4: And I started not going to those places, the mess hall or the recreation room at night or the yard. And I kept to myself in my room.

* * *

AR-36: The first week in C Block, I stayed in my cell. I only went out for one meal a day and I didn't want to bother with anyone. I would go to work and come back straight to my cell.

Isolation, caused by fear of sexual pressure, can cut some men off from the constructive programs that are designed for their betterment:

A-7: I've almost talked myself into going back to school, but I'm too scared. I have that fear that some guy will get me, and I can't go. When I was working, I was all right, but then I had to quit my job because this other guy was trying something with me too.

For some prisoners, adjusting to prolonged cell time is easier than adjusting to the physical presence of aggressors. Isolation, bad as it may seem, restores personal equilibrium. Choosing isolation themselves, men not only adjust to it but appreciate and value it for the safety and privacy it offers.

SOCIAL RELATIONS

After being troubled by a sexual approach—or even if they just feel afraid of sexual approaches—men can become suspicious and distrustful of other prisoners, seeing them as potential aggressors ready to pounce on them. By decreasing their human contacts, these inmates reason, they are decreasing their vulnerability. Global suspicion is the unfortunate result.

ARE-7: If they talk to me, then I have the feeling, "What does he want and what is he after?" Lots of guys I work with will offer you something and then automatically I think, "What does he want or what is he after?"

* * *

AR-10: You can't be open and honest with people here because everyone has got a little game going. No matter how honest an individual is to a person in here, it is a game to the extent that you don't find very many people here that are real. When I do run into someone who wants to talk to me, I do try to keep the conversation to a minimum. Certainly my experience with inmates being friendly is not just their wanting to talk to be friendly. There seems to be ulterior motives there. So that's why I just usually don't talk to people.

Part of adjusting to prison, for all men, not just targets, is learning who to associate with because you need them and who to stay away from because they can harm you. After learning how prison players try to score, i.e., by making friends with their targets, doing them favors, and then "slipping slick maneuvers under their belts," some men will cut themselves off from all possible companionship. They can internalize distrust to such an extent that it becomes a generic attitude change, lasting through their sentences and possibly beyond:

A-7: That will always stay with me. That has always been with me since I've come in here and gone through that experience. That's what I'm afraid of all the time. That's why I won't trust anyone anymore. Because they're sly about it and they slide right in there.

* * *

R-6: I don't think I am really being myself. I think I am not being a real self because I can't be my real self in here. If I was my real self I would manage to speak like Mister Nice Guy out on the street. And some people would take advantage of me, and that is the biggest thing. This is why I am defensive now. It is, like, if I do any favors for anybody, they will take advantage of it.

Suspicion and distrust of others is part of the social learning process in prison. Sexual incidents make a contribution as does the standard advice given to men who look like they may be targets: "Don't accept gifts or favors," "Friendly men are players running a game," etc. Some men, inner-directed, ignore this advice. Others, however, lost in unfamiliar surroundings, take this sort of guidance very much to heart. Staying away from others can become a policy responsive to one's perceived fragility as well as to social norms and peer influence.

AC-10: When I came from reception in Sing-Sing, someone there told me that I would have to be very careful who I talked to, and that I would find out that a lot of inmates would try and be my friend, and then you find out that all they are doing is spreading gossip or rumors. And so the best thing that you can do is try not to talk to anyone and not associate with anyone. Stay to yourself as much as you can. So that even when I came in here that was what I was trying to do.

Lack of trust has its costs. How can a gregarious man with a life sentence survive without friends? When the drive for safety cuts one off from others, one must suffer in loneliness. Self-imposed solitude can prevent one from gaining companionship. It can eliminate supportive ties that help reduce the anxiety connected with fear:

AC-10: I was beginning to feel that you can't really talk to anybody: There's no one that you really can talk with. Even just to clear your head, to air things and to be able to relieve the tension that you feel.

Prison is a man's home and community; most essential needs must be satisfied with the resources men find behind the walls. When one needs people but cuts oneself off from them, victimization is standing in the way of psychological survival. For example, we interviewed a 19-year-old black, an urban target, serving a life sentence, who was used to being with others on the street and found his self imposed isolation hard to bear, although necessary:

ARE-2: I just got tired of people confronting me with it, you know. I can't talk to nobody in here unless it's about sex. And I get tired of talking about sex. I'm really a friendly person and I get along with anyone. My character was changing. If I feel like I can't talk to nobody unless it's about sex, then I don't want to talk to nobody. I have a long time to be here. And if I have to be here for a long time, I might as well get to know somebody, because I can't do it by myself. And there is kids in here that I can talk to without sex being the main part of the conversation. But then again it leads to that inevitably. And then I don't talk to them anymore. Because he was just thinking about that. And then I stay in my cell.

Cutting oneself off from others can boomerang. Aggressors tend to hit on weak-looking men who are alone and look resourceless. Avoiding other inmates, seemingly a protective move, may increase one's risk. The drive toward isolation and the development of suspicion may result in the creation of a public image attractive to aggressors. Unless a man meets a group from his home neighborhood or prisoners known from serving a previous sentence, he must mingle in prison if he hopes to be part of a clique that will offer him physical security and psychic support. A man who becomes a target partly because he enters prison with neither "homie" nor ethnic support, can thus further increase his risk when isolation and suspicion keep him alone:

ARE-4: One guy will tell this guy, "Oh, this guy is no good— stay away from him. He is not wrapped too tight," or something like this and it runs right down the line. Before you know it, you are being completely ignored and you are alone and this is the worst place in the world to be alone.

* * *

AC-10: If you are by yourself, those are the people that turn out to be real preys of those other people. Because the guy who is a loner, they know that he doesn't have anyone to run to his aid if anything starts.

Sexual aggression causes men to band together for protection. Fear promotes the growth of cliques and gangs, which may be defensive groups with exclusive memberships. Whites in New York State prisons generally band together, fearful of blacks. Threat of sexual abuse is part of that fear. By seeing outsiders as potential enemies, feelings about others can become related to who is in the "safe" group and who is outside the group. One impact of the target experience can be the influence on targets of the groups they join for protection. To the extent prison socializes men to support criminal behavior, sexual aggression, by forcing group cohesion, may contribute to criminality.

Social capability, the ability to become a member of a group offering protection, is especially important in determining whether one's coping style will tend toward isolation or toward group involvement. Both styles, however, reflect similar feelings: fear, distrust, and suspicion of others. Both styles separate men from true community involvement: one by restricting them to the walls of a single cell; the other by cementing the barriers of a tight peer group. Life is enriched by contact with others. Sexual aggression by limiting associations, interferes with the quality of a man's daily existence.

RACIAL ATTITUDES

As we have seen, most aggressors are nonwhite and most targets are white. Targets tell us that they grow to hate nonwhites as a result of their experiences. Generalizing their feelings about specific aggressors to the aggressors' ethnic group, targets talk about deep racial prejudice developing. Fueled by fear, by whites' relative weakness in prison, reinforced by anger and violence, racism is a corollary of the target experience:

C2-27: When I was on the streets, I knew a few and when I saw them it was, "How are you, Brothers." And we shook hands. But in here I don't even like to talk to them. I'm sure that they're all evil and I don't like them. They stink. They're all sick. If I had the chance I would really try to do something to them. It's intense. And the only way that I can see for them to do something about it is to make segregated jails. There is so much pressure in here. The blacks—I can't even talk to them. I have nothing but hate for them.

And so I figure that the day that I get out, then I don't know, I don't know what it's going to be like to free myself. I may be going down the road and see a nigger and try to hit him or run over him. I might say that he's one of them. And I know now that I can't talk to any blacks. They're all the same to me. There may be one or two of them that are all right, but they're all the same to me.

* * *

C2-37: All the time, all I could think about was killing them niggers because of their attitude towards the white dudes. Every time a nigger sees a white dude, they say, "I am going to make him my kid." That kind of stuff really makes me sick. I just want to kill them all.

White targets who tell us they come to hate all blacks as a result of sexual incidents claim no prior prejudice while on the street. They see victimization as having changed their attitudes about race. However, it may be that other factors in prison life are equally responsible for this change in racial attitude. Men who tell us that target experiences cause them to hate all blacks may have been prejudiced all along. The general resentment all inmates feel as a result of incarceration may be focused by some whites upon blacks. Targets forced to live in close proximity with different ethnic groups may find blacks offensive simply because they are different from themselves. Nonetheless, we still must consider the surface value of targets' statements that incidents themselves have altered their view of blacks:

C2-46: I used to work with the blacks and I really liked them. I really trusted them and they helped me and everything. I had a friend; I used to go over to his house and play with his little girl and his little boy and everything. And we would get together once in awhile. But now I have the attitude that it will be a long time, even on the outside, before I ever trust one again . . . ever.

           *   *   *

C2-52: I was never prejudiced on the streets and there was this black family—only one black family where I come from—and I used to hang around with them. And when I got in Elmira, man, I started getting prejudiced. Now I don't talk to niggers.

Attitudes About Violence

In Chapter 3, I explored the topic of target violence. As we have seen, men told us they came to prison with nonviolent attitudes but they learned in prison that their former ways were a liability to survival. They described learning to act tough and learning to look tough in order to deter aggressors. We have viewed this, in the chapter on target violence, as a part of the socialization that occurs in confinement. Men I interviewed saw encounters with aggressors as a major force leading them to believe that they must be violent in order to survive. Although we should be cautious in extrapolating behavior change from attitude change, in some cases there seems to be a clear line between believing in violence and acting violently:

C2-45: If someone wrote to one of my friends and told him, explained to him what I am like in jail, he would write and laugh at them. Because they would say that Bob ain't like that at all. He is a great person and you know he would do anything for anybody. He don't fight. He never fought in his life. I am a violent person now, I would fight anybody. I don't give a shit—not no more. It is necessary, I average maybe one fight a week—maybe two.

* * *

A-4: I am more mature. I am sure of what I can do and what I can't do. I am sure that if a man approaches me I can stick a knife in his heart. Before I couldn't do that—I was 17 years old and I couldn't seem to do it. I didn't have no violence in me. I don't worry about it because I know that I have confidence in myself. I hate thinking this way. But I know that I can do it if the situation should arise. And it is a bad feeling to know that you can do it.

SEXUAL BELIEFS AFFECTING IMPACT

Because of the physical setting, much of what we call sexual aggression never goes beyond rough talk or relatively mild physical encounters. Nonetheless, targets react strongly to these messages. In part, their reactions are linked to sexual ideas and beliefs. For example, a theme running through our interviews is fear of forcible sodomy. In spite of the official presence, many see this prospect as a horrifying possibility. Part of this panic and dread is based on belief that the victim of a sexual assault suffers a permanent loss of masculinity. The argot term for homosexual virginity is "manhood" or "hood." Some see losing manhood as the ultimate danger, which they view as unalterable transfiguration.

ARE-4: I wasn't going to be a changed man. And I don't want to walk out of here and be a homosexual. No way in the world.

* * *

C2-45: I wouldn't be no good to my son—I couldn't face him know- ing that they actually took it without me wanting to give it. Forcing me to give my manhood is—anyone would tell you—you would rather die.

* * *

C2-9: If someone came up to me and told me that they were going to take me off, I would try my best to kill him because if I don't I lose everything that I have got.

* * *

A-7: I know darn well that if I become one, I could do my whole bit with no sweat. Just as easy as can be. This is true. Because as long as you came across, nobody would bother you. You'd be well protected. This I would know ahead of time. I would have everything that I wanted. But I could not turn around and walk out in that street in this other world and face my people knowing that I'd done this. And face a woman and marry a woman knowing that I had done this. Possibly there is changes that homos go through that when they become a homo they don't want to know a girl again. But I don't want this to hap- pen to me. I'll stay with my regular life and this is it.

Another belief that goes into the impact of the target experience is the myth of the powerful and successful aggressor. We have seen no cases outside of gang rapes where aggressor strategies really paid off. Nonetheless, the myth widely prevalent among prisoners is that most varieties of sexual aggression pay off in erotic rewards. This myth is a misunderstanding affecting both aggressor and target be- havior. Some aggressors thus act violently when their expectations of success are snubbed. Some targets collapse emotionally because they expect that threats must lead inevitably to sexual exploitations.

AR-41: They, [the aggressors] see that the guy [target] wasn't get- ting no visits and no money from home and so forth. They would come up and furnish the tobacco and cigarettes. He [target] realizes that he can't pay back and at first the guy will say, "Okay." Then he comes back maybe a month later with another carton and he says, "The last time it was all right." But after the second or third time he tells him that you owe me some money and that is when this all starts up.
    And he says, "Well, a little sex act and we will be even." And the guy is scared that he is going to hurt him because he [aggressor] might say, "Well I am going to cut you if I

don't get my money." And the guy is scared and so forth. A lot of people there realize that you don't go to the police because you could end up getting killed or messed up or something. And so the guy just goes and says, "Okay," and that is it.

* * *

CR-5: The guy comes in and two or three guys get together. They see him in the shower and, "Wow," they think, "I wouldn't mind getting down to him." And so they wait for the guy. Then they walk up to him, especially if it is a young kid, they go directly to him and they tell him that they are going to give him this. They just talk to him and they find out what kind of a person he is. They see that he is a kid and he is ignorant of this ever happening in the system at all. He is just ever so weak. And they are sure to get him, you know, slowly but surely.

* * *

CR-29: I told him, "Don't go their way. They are going to be offering you candy, cigarettes. They are going to get you into gambling and they are going to get you into debt." They got another dude here and he is in debt for about 70 crates and he can't pay so they are looking for a shot of life. So he is trying to cut himself up and really injure himself bad so that he can get out of here and be shipped out of here. Those things you just don't fool around with because they are going to get you one way or the other.

The myth of success comprises the standard scenario of victimization: The target accepts gifts that are interpreted by aggressors as loans implying the lender's right to sexual access. Once the victim accepts these gifts, his fate as a victim is sealed. In our study there is only a single incident where the scenario was played out. The importance of the story lies in the fact that it is believed, not that it is true.

Dislike of homosexuality, in the case of straight targets, also contributes to the emotional impact of victimization. Most men come to prison with staunch taboos and traditions against homosexuality. Their stand is more a moral belief than a statement of personal preference. They hate homosexuals as others, important to them, hate homosexuals. And they do not view sex among men as casual behavior but as activity marking a man with a deviant identity: a homosexual is a "queer." When one is propositioned or attacked for sex, one can feel labeled a "faggot." Anger and emotional uneasiness reflect, in part, distain for homosexuality:

AR-23: This guy thinks that I am a homo or a punk kid that he could fuck me. I think it was my own hang-ups—there wasn't that much fear mixed in with it. No physical fear. Except for the normal physical fear that you would have if you were going to fight somebody, like you might get hurt, but I consider that normal. The thing was homosexuality, in my head. This guy was trying to fuck me and I was hung up over that.

* * *

C2-53: I myself don't like homosexuality. If one guy comes up to me—I mean a homosexual—if one had come up to me and he wanted me to perform a sex act on him, I would try to kill the dude. I beat the heck out of one homosexual that had come towards me.

* * *

APC-11: This is just something that you don't do—that is not right even though you are locked up in here the rest of your life—to me, this is just not right.

FLOUNDERING FOR SOLUTIONS

Because targets struggle awkwardly to extricate themselves from their perceived fate, because they stumble and hesitate, the impact of the experience is increased beyond what it would be if the problem could be addressed smoothly. Doubt, indecision, not knowing what to do, and mulling over equally distasteful options, drag out the incident and intensify its emotional shock. We coded interviews for the presence or absence of "floundering," i.e., for statements about confusion, paralysis and inability to respond, or loss of control of the situation. Using this definition, floundering occurred in about a quarter of the incidents. For example:

APC-11: I shut the door when he would come up and start bothering me. I was trying to tell him that I don't do these things. He is trying to tell me that it is not going to bother me, and it won't hurt at all.
So I am saying, "You know, I don't want to do that."
And he says, "Well, you are going to have to."

Talking to that one guy, it just seemed as though he couldn't see my viewpoint. I was going to tell the guards a couple of times but then I thought—well, maybe I had better not because they would find out and then maybe I would have a whole gang after me.

They just started bothering me a little bit more, and I have never been in a fight in my life, but if anybody tried I would just have to hurt them. I wouldn't want to have to hurt nobody—I don't want nothing like that to happen. Getting him to leave me alone, I said, "Let me think about it." Because I was scared, really scared. He would go away for awhile. Then come back a little while later. When I was afraid I wanted to go into Protection, I wanted to talk to somebody.

Failing to take action can lead to aggressors continuing their approaches. Inmates who are generally nonassertive have a special problem because their attempts to communicate resistance bogs down. Yet, even the most forceful "no" often gets targets nowhere. As they look for other solutions, targets can become disturbed because all available options seem to have strong arguments against them: Ignoring aggressors or doing nothing wounds one's pride and may encourage overtures; fighting will get you in trouble with the authorities and make a dangerous enemy of the aggressors; and one doesn't talk to staff because they want inmates to rat out. The feeling that something must be done combined with the fact that one doesn't know what to do, adds to the turmoil of the target experience:

C2-47: Well, the one thing that I was thinking about was escaping. The other thing that I was thinking about was fighting and going over and saying to this guy, "Look—if you want me, let's get it on and get it settled right here and now." And the other thing I was saying in my mind was if I fight this guy, this is going to happen if I do fight him and that is going to happen if I don't fight him. So a lot of things told me to go to the C.O. And if you go to the C.O., it is not good in prison. It is not good at all because they can help you. Sure, they can help you, but they are going to harm you in the long run.

* * *

AR-36: I was helpless. I had to sit there and there was nothing that I could do about it. I started to figure out what the consequences would be if I didn't make an aggressive move back and make the guy back up. Then I kept on trying to think how much that would magnify the situation. By building up and building up I would actually have to hurt the guy. And I wasn't sure. What I was trying to do was to try and understand what the best way was. I just couldn't come up with anything.

* * *

ARE-1: This may sound funny, but sex in a way is a hard thing for me to talk about, and I am in here for rape. Even when I first was talking with Miss Morris [his therapist] about my problems and stuff, it was actually hard to say rape or sex or anything like that. It is hard for me to talk about homo stuff even when someone brings it up down on the block or something. It is hard to bring the word homo out.

CONCLUSION

Fear is the most commonly mentioned emotion accompanying the target experience. Fear can be a general feeling or a specific apprehension of being physically harmed, sexually assaulted, or killed. Fear can shift from the arena of the incident and its players to encompass feelings about the entire prison milieu. Fear is intensified by targets' inability to remove themselves from the presence of agressors easily, and by their propensity to worry about the consequences of aggressive moves. Regardless of the level of force in an incident, fear can be an intense emotion, persisting over time and governing subsequent life-styles. Not all men emerge from incidents feeling fearful. About 50 percent of our targets said they did, although we suspect underreporting. And the shape of the targets' fear differs from target to target, depending on their personal characteristics.

Anger is also a common reaction, and includes accumulated frustration resulting from persistent unwanted approaches. Men who have trouble controlling feelings are particularly sensitive to this response. Other prisoners are likely to be vulnerable because confinement causes frustration to which the unwanted sexual approach contributes. Anger can result in explosive reactions or can be narrowly held in check, added to the inmate's tension and anxiety.

Anxiety was reported for about one third of the incidents. The stress accompanying this tension frequently was signaled by physical indicators. Fear was the primary feeling bringing on anxiety, which could persist far beyond the end of the incident. Men with previous mental health problems seemed particularly vulnerable.

Crises can follow from sexual approaches as men react to their fear. These crises are commonly signaled by emotional upset along with requests for medication or isolation. Suicidal thoughts and gestures sometimes accompany these crises when men feel their fate as future victims is sealed or when men wish staff to move them to a safe area.

There is an impact on social relations. Men's lives are disrupted and they commonly end up isolating themselves to avoid contact with aggressors. Men also join with others to form defensive groupings.

Racial attitudes are affected, with men saying that they come to hate nonwhites as a result of their experiences. Attitudes toward violence are also affected and men report that they become more violent after being targets.

The impact of sexual aggression seems to be accentuated by inmate beliefs that sexual assault leads to permanent identity change, that aggressors are successful, and that homosexual activity is reprehensible. These beliefs add to the intensity of the target experience.

The social and psychological impacts described in this chapter extend to all targets of sexual aggression, regardless of the level of force in incidents. There is no clear association between the amount of violence deployed in an incident and the intensity of the target reaction. However, since sexual assault may be thought of as a special circumstance, victims of prison rape will be discussed separately in the following chapter.

Victims of Prison Rape

 The experiences of male rape victims are the topic of this chapter. Although the prison literature is replete with comments about sexual assault, our interviews for the first time provide extensive clinical material about the male rape victim. Without much evidence, it has been customary to assign to prison rape victims an imaginative list of consequences. Weiss and Friar (1975), for example, state one of the most common assumptions: "Repeated homosexual rape causes the inmate victims to develop a new sexual identity. They now harbor a raped female in their male bodies" (p. 74). Other ideas include the notion that victims become willing "kids" of prison "daddies" and that recidivism can be linked to embitterment engendered by prison victimization (Davis 1968a,b; Weiss and Friar, 1975). These assumptions lack empirical underpinnings.

We looked at 15 incidents of sexual assault. Only one of these men came from the random sample (which included over 80 subjects), leading to the conclusion that sexual assaults in New York State prisons are rare relative to less severe target–aggressor encounters. However, were we to assume that one out of 80 over a 12-month period was a reliable estimate, then this rate would be about seven times higher than the rate of rape for women in the free world. In 1975, for example, according to victim surveys, the nationwide rate of heterosexual rape was 1.7 per 1000 women (U.S. Department of Justice, 1977). Norming our figures to correspond with these yields a rate of 12.5 per 1000 male prisoners.

The possibility of rape adds to the intensity of all types of target experience, since most prisoners know about rapes occurring in the institutions where they are living. As a consequence, many inmates perceive themselves to be living in a dangerous environment. The occasional occurrence of sexual assault also tells us about a type of behavior that is likely to occur if security is relaxed.

A CASE OF SEXUAL ASSAULT

We have mentioned that prison rape is an unusual event. Yet, during the inevitable complexity of institutional life, aggressors are always waiting to move in. Atypical situations allowing rape to occur are certain to happen at times. The following case illustrates this:

The victim, a new inmate, was transferred to the prison mental hospital for evaluation. Placed on an open dormitory where about 40 men live, no special classification procedures recognized his potential for victimization. Guards may have been indifferent and the dormitory was dominated by a gang of aggressors who routinely assaulted all young white men. The incident is not representative of normal conditions; rather, it illustrates what can occur when official security procedures break down. The target, a middle-class, 19-year-old man from a Long Island suburb, tells us what happened:

C2-16: The sex pressure started the second day. Some guy came in and said, "You owe for cigarettes, man, and do you want to give up your ass tonight?"

And, I said, "No, man, and anybody that comes in here talking about that I am going to hit him with a chair or something." So, then I seen them doing it to kids at night that were scared. I was thinking of taking a mayonnaise jar and breaking it in half in case they tried it against me—and using it as a weapon. But then I was thinking if I do that then I will get more time and that is all I could think of—more time. And I did not want to get more time.

Well, I was lying on the bed and I was half awake and half asleep. It was hard to sleep that night because the officers would not keep these guys in their room. After 10 o'clock you are supposed to be in your room. Because there aren't any doors, they can walk the halls all night. They came when I was sleeping and one guy shook me and he said, "Come with me to the room." And I said that I was not going no place. And then this one guy who weighed about 240 pounds started twisting my arm—and it really started to hurt. And I figured that this guy would really break my arm, so I am going to do it. And that was that. They took me in a room that was two rooms away from where I was. They closed the door and a couple of them stood outside to see if the officer came by.

So I went into the room and I lied on the bed and they gave me all this bullshit. They told me that it won't hurt and that I was not a homo and don't worry they won't tell anybody. So, I had about two or three guys that were hanging on top of me and I was very upset that night.

I was in there about 20 minutes because I did not scream or anything. I just let them do it and that was it. These guys—they work very fast. They just get on top of the guy and they do it in like three minutes maybe. So that was that.

I felt depressed. At times, I did think of suicide. I was getting a suicide thought because I say, "Hey, man, I am going to be doing this night after night." Like it was just at the beginning of my time and I had not even gone to my parole board. I was really confused, and I cried at night and I was upset. I was thinking about that—suicide. When you have got four guys every day that are going to fuck you in the ass every night, it is nothing to look forward to.

I never thought about killing anyone or anything in my life, but like I was just thinking about going over with a jar and then hitting him and the whole thing would be over. In that week myself I changed so much. I had all these hostile thoughts. The violent thoughts were that the next time they came over to me I am going to make an example. I am going to take a jar and hit some guy in the back of the head.

I am thinking: What would a real man do in situations like this? I was thinking that I should have taken a chair and I should have just smashed one of these guys. That is what I was thinking because it kept happening over and over. I am thinking if I know these guys they are going to come again, and they are going to screw me and if I let them then I am at fault, if I let it happen and I know it is going to happen then it is my fault.

Well, I was upset because first of all, most guys consider themselves a man, and you always say that in jail no one is ever going to do that to you. I was very upset about it for about four or five months afterwards because I thought that I had lost my manhood.

It was just a very painful thing that happened. You just start to get over it—and you say it was just not my fault. You just say to yourself you were in an abnormal atmosphere and it just happened. That is about the most painful part of my time.

I had thought of telling the officers but they had told me when it happened that if I told the officers—even if I did go to protective keep-lock that they would run a wire on me, and get me in the cell down there. Because this was my first time in jail, and I did not know what was happening.

WHY RAPE CAN OCCUR

Some incidents of rape may occur because proper custodial supervision is lacking, as we have just reviewed. But other assaults occur in closely supervised surroundings. Here, the aggressors work out careful plans to lure the victim to a spot where rape can take place. The victim is a "mark" in a con game. He must be induced to cooperate to a certain point in the incident. In these types of assault, the location where the victim is lured lacks security, so that the incident can take place. To be sure, modern prisons and jails are designed to protect inmates from each other and allow for constant custodial supervision. Nonetheless, aggressors can find ways to circumvent (on rare occasions) the most rigid custodial routines. For example, in one case, the victim was told he could purchase marijuana if he accompanied an aggressor. The aggressor and the victim then walked together through a steel door, which was open for a few minutes to allow a group of inmates to pass through it. Once in the cell block area, other aggressors appeared and dragged the victim under a bed in one of the aggressor's cells. The steel door should have prevented the victim from entering an improper area. Yet, security systems are never in complete effect all of the time, and aggressors learn to circumvent these systems.

A similar incident occurred in a small room off a gym. The officer supervising the gym could not see into this room. The victim was lured into the room by an aggressor who asked him to play handball. The other aggressors were hiding in the room when the victim entered it to change his shoes. In this incident, the victim (an urban black) was an acquaintance of the aggressors, who were urban blacks from his city, and the victim knew beforehand that these men were sexually attracted to him. The victim took no extraordinary measures to protect himself because he believed that the institution would protect him at all times.

Victims of sexual assault are invariably targets of aggressive sexual approaches before they are assaulted. Generally, however, they do not tell staff about these approaches nor do they take any other extraordinary means to protect themselves. They feel a part of the prison subculture or are afraid of retaliation, keeping their problems to themselves. They also tend to feel that the situation is one that they can manage themselves. After all, many inmates are targets but very few become victims. The probability of any target becoming a victim is relatively low. Just as some overreact, believing they will be victims of rape after they become targets of aggressors, others underreact when they are approached. It is true that targets receive warnings before they become rape victims. The problem they must assess is the significance of cues, and they have to estimate their own capabilities:

AU-4: I thought to myself just like what every other inmate thinks. I can handle one or two of them if they want to fuck around with me that much. I can handle one or two of them, you know. But, then it come down to six and then I didn't know what to do.

Inadequate classification is always at issue. In one incident, a 16-year-old defendant was placed with adult sentenced prisoners in a large county jail. The victim complains that:

C2-22: They just stick guys in where they had an opening. Like, say, you just come in, and you didn't have time at all and you are supposed to go on the east side. The west side is for the sentenced guys. I was not sentenced at the time. They put me on the west side and stuck me in the kitchen.

A prison or jail security system may tax the patience of both staff and inmates. Routines established by security minded administrators may appear petty inconveniences to those who must carry them out. For example, inmates are supposed to keep their doors closed at all times. But in some prisons this rule is regularly relaxed to permit a more comfortable atmosphere. An officer faced with a peaceful tier may no longer see sense in warding off the exceptional event the security measure is designed to prevent. The rarity of sexual assault is itself an ingredient in the inevitable entropy overtaking well-planned security systems. The difference between custodial theory and practice explains why some sexual assaults take place.

Once a victim is trapped with no officer around, the most important circumstance allowing the rape is the amount of force or threat of force leveled at the victim by the aggressors. If the setting allows extreme violence to be employed, any man is easily overwhelmed. All rapes in our study were thus carried out by groups of aggressors, often aided by associates who held men but didn't actually assault them:

C2-22: I took a shower that night and all of a sudden I came out of the shower and there was two dudes standing there. And they told me, "Look, man, I have got a knife and we want to see what you have got."

I told them, "Look, I ain't got nothing. I ain't got no candy or cigarettes or nothing like that." I said, "What do you want?" That was the first time I had ever been into a place like that. All of a sudden two of them came in my room and jumped me and this one guy was watching for the officer because they make a watch check every half hour. They told me, "If you call the C.O., we will kill you." And, like, this man had a spoon sharpened.

* * *

ARE-1: I was working and then I got hit in the back of the head. And then five or six guys are holding me down and it didn't take but, say, 60 seconds from the time that I was hit on the head until the time that I was on the floor. There was three of them that did it, but the rest were their friends. You can say that it was rough. Scared, sure you were scared, but it's the realization that there is nothing that you can do about it. You can stand there and fight and fight, but within five minutes they're going to have it. And there is just so much that you can do. There is nothing that you can do about it. And you can throw a few punches and if you're caught totally by surprise then you're through before you start. The numbers alone were enough to defeat me; the surprise, though, didn't help much either.

IMMEDIATE REACTIONS

Physical reactions are generally experienced directly after the event. Along with pain from the rape itself, secondary medical ailments may cause both discomfort and uneasiness:

AU-9: I felt like vomiting—just vomiting—that is all. Like, my insides were destroyed and there was a great deal of pain. Outside of when having bowel movements I passed blood, and I continually had something like diarrhea and I was taking Kaopectate to settle down the diarrhea, but it was still painful.

Worried about physical damage, victims may feel a compelling need for medical help—a need that forces them to share their problem with staff. As one victim tells us, some men are reluctant to ask for aid, but their physical condition forces them to do so.

AU-4: Well, for one I was in all kinds of discomfort. My ass was bleeding and everything. And I was thinking, "I should go to the doctor." And then I said, "No, I can't." And then I said, "I guess I should because it could get infected, and I could get all sick and everything." And what happened, I did get sick. I got real sick. I couldn't even walk hardly. So, I told the lieutenant about it.

The emotional impact, even relatively close to the event, is tied to concern about social stigma.

C2-16: I was upset. Shame. The whole thing was shame. The whole thing.

* * *

C2-22: I was hurting. I mean physically and mentally. Well, then if the man did this here to me, everybody in this institution is going to know about it. I can't walk around and face these people, you know, with this here going on. So, I just like closed myself off from everybody else.

Like other targets, victims of rape experience a personal crisis. But the crisis following rape differs from crises following other target incidents because rape victims are harder pressed to deal with the social meaning of their victimization. Some victims feel that the rape has socially slaughtered them, and that they will be scorned because they will no longer be seen as men. Turned inward, the belief causes victims to despise themselves. Viewing themselves as pariahs, as objects of scorn by their own as well as other's standards, the crises these men go through includes not only fear but self-hate and doubt about future social and self-acceptability:

ARE-1: If I lost again in a situation like that I would step down and hang up. I don't have enough desire to live with myself with another incident like that. I can't and I won't.

* * *

C2-22: I said, "When I get back out on the streets, Man, I am not going to be able to face nobody." So I thought about committing suicide. And so I went down to the shower and took a rope and tied it up and put it around my neck and I was going to jump off.

While there is no evidence that homosexual rape actually causes change of sexual identity, victims are concerned that others will think of them as homosexual. This can cause the victims to assume they will attract more attackers because they see undefended homosexuals as fair game in prison. Similar to other targets, the victims' crises can be increased by fear that they will be victims again. A composite crisis can follow that includes concern about the psychological implications of one's experience:

AU-9: I was thinking, "Wow, my parents." I couldn't even call them but once a month; I just didn't have time to explain anything to them and I just kept saying, "Look, Mom and Dad, I don't think I will ever be able to come back home." That was the only thought that was in my mind; I may die in here.

I despised everyone that I seen. Even those that come up and asked me what happened and what could they do for me. I told them to go to hell, and to drop dead. And, the only thing I thought about was hiding and destroying myself. Like this was the crossing of the bridge, whereas, whom—I am on this side of the fence now. And I am in a world all by myself. I don't want to be like those other people, swishing and walking up and down the galleries, not knowing what is going to happen to me. Now I am in this prison, and the word is going to go around, and it is going to happen again and again and again.

In recovering from rape, men follow strategies congruent with the meaning the event has for them. For example, to the extent that the victims see the rape as an event fixing them into a public role—that of a weak sissy—part of recovery may be to reject that role by putting on an exaggerated tough guy front. A victim's associate describes his behavior after he was raped:

C2-28: He was trying to make himself act like more of a man than what he was before. To me, like, he was all right before, when he talked to me and everything. But, then, after the rape, he tried to act like, well, "I am bigger than you are," and stuff like that. And he just went at it from that angle. And he just went on acting bigger than he was.

Once the initial shock is over, victims look for ways to prevent being raped again as well as ways to restore their self-image. Not surprisingly, some try to establish a fierce demeanor, both as a way of deterring future attacks and as a way of saying to themselves and to others that they are not punks or sissies. In trying to understand why they were raped, the men arrive at the answer that others did not respect them because they had no reputation for violence. As one young victim says, "I kept thinking: What would a real man have done in a situation like that?" This sort of self-doubt can cause victims to act with violence:

AU-9: I sat down and I started to build up my reputation. This may be somewhat psychologically impaired as far as my outlook, but I truly definitely feel that if an individual has had any type of physical contact with an individual of his own nature, he makes a projection somewhat to say, like, "I done it and who is next." I mean, he is prone to this fear that, God, it has happened to me and I wonder if I have this halo on me. So I started walking around, cursing out at individuals and pushing on them and shit like this.

* * *

ARE-1: They had a code in the prison on the chow line that said no man should cut ahead of you in the chow line. And this man passed me a couple of times in the line, and he knew that I was aware of what he was doing. If I failed to do what I was supposed to do here, then I was lost again. So the next day, when they come through the chow line, when this guy cut in front of me, I hit him in the head with a tray as hard as I could. And when he went to the ground, I hit him several more times before the guard could reach me. It is regrettable but it is the only way that you can handle it. And I didn't want to do it, but I did what I had to do to protect myself. It was self-preservation, the first law of nature. I had to do it.

I would fall prey to anyone who had the strength—who thought they had the strength to defeat me. And if I hadn't done something there to boost my own mental morale, it would have been much easier to do. I had to increase my own mental morale because I couldn't walk around the yard without fearing what would happen to me. And I had to do something. And that was approximately about a week and a half after the incident in the powerhouse [the rape].

Seeking safety, some men also prepare to fight to protect their reputation.

AU-9: The word had got around what had happened, so the individual who had befriended me says, "Yeah, man, they are down and the word is spread." And I said, "So what, I am ready for them now. I can fight in here and by the time they get back they won't be so wise. I will get some razor blades together and things, you know, and the first dude that walks up to me . . ." This was the feeling that I continually had—if I am going to die, let me take one of them with me.

Prison rape victims alter their life-styles as much as they do their behavior toward others. Like other targets, they often enter protective housing after the incident. Some occupy safe niches in the prison where they are doing time. Most of these efforts are successful in stopping subsequent victimization: Victims are generally victims only once. The circumscribed manner in which they live after being attacked prevents repeated attacks. In no case in our sample did the reactions of victims extend to their becoming homosexual partners of aggressors or other men.

LONG-RANGE EFFECTS

Victims continue to be affected months after the event. Flashbacks of the incident may cause crying spells. Nausea may occur sporadically. Victims report being generally bothered by memories of their rape. Some seek psychiatric aid in attempts to cope with what they initially perceive as a new identity. Others find it difficult to perform as they are expected to.

AU-4: That has been fucking with me. That fucked me for about two months. Every time I get a little thought about it—about that knife coming up in the air or something—it is a flashback. I think of that knife up to my throat, and stuff, and I get in my cell and will be thinking about it sometimes and I will start crying.

I was actually sick. I was sick to my stomach all the time because of what happened. I started thinking about it, and I would get nauseated. I would feel like I had to puke up but I never puked up. I think about it at night in my cell here. Yeah, tears come to my eyes and stuff like that, but I don't talk about it to nobody, and I don't say nothing to nobody about it.

*   *   *

C2-22: It has fucked my head up quite a bit. I still got it in my head now: I will be down and reading a book in my room and this will go through my mind and it will blow my mind apart. I will say, "Damn, I have to start thinking about this fucking shit again." I want to forget it and say past is past.

Managing stigma—or potential stigma—is a long-range concern of male rape victims. These men worry a great deal about what will happen if others find out what they have experienced:

C2-22: I got a girl out there with a kid and, like, I don't tell her nothing. She don't even know that this happened. Like I said before, I was embarrassed. If I ever told her what happened, I don't know what would go through her mind. . . . You see, because, if I tell her, I am afraid that she is just going to pack up and leave and take the kid and go on their way. If I keep it hidden with her, then things might be better off.

*   *   *

AU-4: I was thinking, "What if guys come down here from Elmira and see me down here and start saying that I am a homo?" I couldn't go for that. I was thinking, "What if I go back out in the streets?" Because I told my father about it. I told my father what happened. I was thinking, "If I go back on the street, will my father accept what has happened to me?"

The victim of a prison sexual assault finds it difficult to reintegrate himself into prison society. Other inmates (and staff) may misunderstand the event and assume the victim of a sexual assault "gives it up" willingly. Being labeled a homosexual is a dismaying condition for most young working-class men. Victims may worry about having a future and may contemplate suicide as they see themselves facing scorn wherever they go. Socially dislocating incidents (secondary victimization) may occur in the months following the assault. The victim may overreact to perceived approaches, and may precipitate fights to stop what he views as another assault in progress. Victims may also fight with men who taunt them. If they have sought staff aid, they may feel that others will assume that the victim has told authorities the names of his aggressors, so that the victim will not only be viewed a "punk" and a "pussy," but also a "rat":

AU-9: I go inside to sick call and he sits over across from me and says, "Hello, Miss Brown." I didn't do nothing. I go and ignore him. I had a book with me and I was reading. He pushes my book down and I says, "What is your bag, man?" and he says, "I heard about you, you are sweet, real good." And I looked at him like he wasn't even fucking talking to me and he said, "Are you trying to boof me out. I know you are a homo." And, I said, "Look, man." And then I got up and I hit him and I knocked him down. And the officer runs over and he says, "What is the matter?" And I said, "This punk tried right here and I am going to bust his jaw." And the guy says, "You are a fag, you are a fag." And the officer is sitting here and he says, "Look, Brown, you got to stay out of trouble—this is about your fifth fight." "I don't want these punks harassing me," I told him.

* * *

AU-4: This guy comes up to me while I was in Albion. He was one of the guys that was in on it. They shipped him down there with me, and I didn't know that it was him because I couldn't identify all the guys. I identified three of them. And he says to me, "Man, you did that for us and you did it for nothing, man—you is a homo." And I go to him, "Hey, man, stay away from me because if you don't, I am going to drop a dime on you and get you shipped out of here." And he said, "Man, you can't do that—you ain't got enough heart." And I says, "Oh, yeah." And I walked right over to the administration building and told them about it, about him being down there, so they sent me to camp, to Camp Monterey. That added to it, thinking that he might spread something around, a wire around in that institution, and he did. He talked to two guys, and he told them about it. Those guys started to give me problems too. They say all kinds of things. Like when I walked by: "Hey, you homo. . . . He's a homo." "Are you a homo?" All sorts of shit, so that was added to it.

The interviews fail to show long-term, permanent effects of the experience on victims with the exception of some men testifying that they became more violent as a result of the experience. At first, victims worry about their sexual identity. As time goes on, however, they learn sexual assault does not alter one's commitment to heterosexuality. It appears that eventually the trauma of the event wears thin. Men report being bothered by thoughts of the incident for months and years afterward, but they are able to cope with this memory, which is not disabling. Eventually, even while the victims are still in prison, they restore order to their social lives. The crisis following sexual assault declines sharply with time and is most acute at the time of the event. The psychic recovery of the victim is essentially complete after a period of months:

C2-16: It was upsetting and everything but, like, the way I look at it, in jail anything can happen. I have seen guys really hurt in jail, so I figure it is not anything to be ashamed of. I have accepted jail as an abnormal atmosphere where they have guys in here that have murdered people and have carved and chopped people. I figure that the worst thing is if you are cut because if you are cut you have to wear that for life. This is something that is cruel and unfortunate, but I can put it out of my head. It is not a physical thing that you have to wear for life.

*   *   *

AU-4: I started looking at these people like these guys are going to help. I started talking to them more and more and more. And I come out of the nutshell that I was in. I am trying to keep it off my mind, and I am trying to have fun and be happy with people, and be nice to people, and that way I have kept it off my mind.

If we can detect a long-range effect of prison rape in our interviews, it is that the experience of being a victim trains men *to raise* the level of violence they have been accustomed to employing. In this regard, the effect of being a rape victim is similar to the effect of being any type of sexual target. Statements like the following, from a rape victim, clearly show victimization leading to lower thresholds for violent behavior and explosiveness.

ARE-1: I would walk around a corner and I would wonder if something was going on. If the corner was over here then I was over there and making sure that nobody was behind me. And I constantly carried a weapon and I got into fights. But they didn't try it anymore because they knew that I was carrying a weapon. And I had a sadistic attitude at the time, and I didn't care anymore. When you don't care, it don't matter how many people that you chop, you just try to get as many as you can, if they come at you. And this is the only way to solve something like this. But it hurt me just as much to have the attitude that I had as to have the attitude of weakness. So, even the attitude that "I'm going to kill this dude when he comes up to me," that doesn't help at all. Because when I got out in society I had the same attitude and it took me years to get over that attitude.

Even though I defeated fear with hate, I destroyed myself. When I came out of the penitentiary, it was sickening. If somebody would say hello to me, and they would say it in the wrong frame of voice, it was—it was terrible. I knew why I was doing it, and I couldn't stop it. You can control hate and you can control fear, but if you come to the point whre it controls you, then either way you're losing.

When I first came out of prison, I lost a job because of something that I said to the boss. The boss said something that I didn't like, so right away, without even thinking about it, I told him, "Hey, look if you want to square off, then let's go out and get some wood and square off. But, leave me alone otherwise." And that is bad when you come out and you can't control yourself. It's no good. That is bad as having a fear of the penitentiary. I lost control of myself.

As we have seen, prison rape, as well as other forms of sexual aggression, has a significant impact on prisoners who are targets of this behavior. The reaction to sexual victimization includes psychological trauma and social maladjustment. As seen in the above interview, sexual aggression can also precipitate violence on the part of targets. However, knowing target reactions only partially explains our topic. To understand these events more fully, we must examine the prison sexual aggressors.

Aggressors

The report by Davis (1968b) prompted Susan Brownmiller (1975) to declare, "Homosexual rape in the Philadelphia prisons turned out to be a microcosm of the female experience with heterosexual rape" (p. 102). In general, our information confirms Brownmiller's statement. The explanation for prison sexual aggression closely follows explanations for rape in the free world. My aim here is to describe prison aggressors, compare them to heterosexual rapists on the street, and discuss causal theories common to both.

My method is statistical in that I have analyzed the tabulated background characteristics of identified prison aggressors and a randomly selected comparison group. My method is also clinical in that I examined interviews held with individuals. As I described in Chapter 1, I located 45 aggressors through careful search. The sample was not random and may not be representative. But this technique was the only way I could have accumulated an aggressor study group. I classified 17 aggressors as "sexual assaulters": They were convicted in courts for sodomizing fellow prisoners, or were found guilty in prison disciplinary proceedings. The others (28 of 45) are classified as "sexual pressurers": In approaching their targets, they used threats or force, but no actual rape took place. Finding the backgrounds of sexual pressurers markedly similar to those of sexual assaulters, I pooled these two groups to facilitate analysis. Aggressor backgrounds were then compared to the backgrounds of other prisoners in Attica and Coxsackie. For some factors, such as race, the Department furnished me with data about the entire population. For other factors, such as family background, I gathered the data myself from a randomly selected comparison group.

RESEARCH HYPOTHESIS: The Subculture of Violence

Most theories of male sexual aggression, as explanations, are tentative and problematical. Some interpretations of the behavior remain totally unverified. Other hypotheses have only been tested with facts from rapists in treatment programs, generally men with unusual psychological conditions (M. Cohen, 1971). This approach runs against the common observation that most rapists have "normal" personalities, failing to qualify for psychiatric labels mandating special treatment.

One problem in this area of research is that few men are readily open about illegal, immoral, and perverse acts. Just as it has inhibited other work on this topic, informant reticence hampered my endeavor. Ultimately, as a result, I limited the systematic portion of my inquiry to testing an hypothesis with background factors from institutional files rather than with interviews. This hypothesis is Amir's explanation for forcible rape, or the subcultural interpretation of sexual aggression.

Amir's Theory of Sexual Aggression

Amir (1971), presenting statistics showing the similarity of rapists to other violent offenders, applies to sexual aggression ideas set out by Wolfgang and Ferracuti in *The Subculture of Violence* (1967): A subculture in our midst carries values and traditions supporting aggression. Norm adoption is one psychological process linking the background variables (proving subcultural membership) to the aggressive activity with which they are correlated. Another psychological motive thought to direct subcultural members toward aggression is compulsive masculinity: Lacking male identity figures in the home and lacking access to economic or educational indices of status, some lower-class males turn to outward toughness to prove their masculinity to themselves and others (Toby, 1966).

When Amir looks to "subculture" to explain rape, he mainly looks to a group made up of young, lower-class males. His subcultural interpretation of forcible rape makes sexual aggression part of overall patterns of violence carried out by these individuals. Believing the subculture of violence thesis best explains most sexual aggression, Amir (1971) offers the following proof for his position:

1. Sexual aggression prevails in the same subculture in which other types of violence prevail.
2. The rates of rape are highest among the same group that produces the highest rates for other violent crime, i.e., black, single, young, lower-class males.
3. Many of those arrested for rape had been previously arrested for other crimes against persons.
4. The incidence of group rape shows that rape often unfolds in the context of a peer group, where it is learned along with other violent behavior.
5. Descriptive studies indicate values supporting sexual aggression are part of the subculture of violence.

Let us turn to the characteristics of our aggressors to see if they support Amir's position.

CHARACTERISTICS OF AGGRESSORS

Age

In respect to age, prison aggressors are prototypical of rapists in America. Among our aggressors, for instance, 46 percent were 19 or under (as compared to 44 percent of the heterosexual rapists in Amir's study). Our prison aggressor group was significantly younger than the comparison group. This corroborates the earlier observation that sexual aggression is most intense in youth institutions. When classification schemes place all adolescents and young adults together, high rates of sexual aggression result because most aggressors tend to be youths. Studies, in addition to Amir's, show a marked tendency for sexual aggressors in free society to follow this pattern. Radzinowicz (1957), for example, found 37 percent of one group of convicted rapists to be under 21 years old. The FBI placed 25 percent of rapists arrested in the 20- to 24-year-old group and 31 percent in the 15- to 19-year old group (U.S. Dept. of Justice, 1960). Youth is one factor thought to distinguish the subculture of violence in America, for the age of sexual aggressors closely parallels that of all other violent offenders. Why do young men tend to be more violent than others? Wolfgang and Ferracuti (1967) suggest that "physically aggressive behavior for this group converges with notions about the masculine ideal" (p. 258). If prison sexual aggression is a way of demonstrating masculinity, then we would expect to find it occurring during youth, when identity forming processes are most acute. We should also consider that youths are more likely than others to form groups that behave violently. Thus, it should come as no surprise that a large percentage of the incidents in our study were carried out by multiple aggressors. Like youthful street gangs, prison rape gangs carry cultural norms encouraging the use of force, norms which, given the fact of group membership, influence youths (more than adults) regardless of individual psychologies. Also, we should consider that youth is a time of heightened sexual interest. Because of the reasons linking sexual aggression to youth, most aggressors probably mature out of such behavior by their mid-twenties.

Race

Discussing correlations between race and violent crime can be painful for speaker and listener alike. Following a lecture on racial patterns in prison sexual aggression, a black student once told me, "You know, man, while you were talking about that, I felt like crawling under the desk or something." Indeed, knowing that the topic offends minorities and that findings can be misinterpreted to support racist notions, one is tempted to ignore or deemphasize the tendency of blacks to be sexual aggressors in prison. But we cannot do this. In prison, race often identifies culture. We conclude culture provides the key to explaining sexual aggression in prison. Let us make it clear it is not black culture that is behind prison sexual aggression; rather, it is a criminal, male, youthful, black subculture of violence.

Our findings with respect to ethnicity support the subcultural hypothesis. Aggressors tend to be black out of proportion to the representation of blacks in the prison population: While about 50 percent of the populations of the prisons we studied are black, 78 percent of the aggressors are black. The same fact holds true for other prisons. In Davis' study (1968b), for example, 85 percent of the aggressors in 129 incidents were black.

Heterosexual aggressors in free society also tend to be black out of proportion to the percentage of blacks in the population. Concerning the 1960 Uniform Crime Reports, Amir states, "Negroes comprise 53 percent of all persons arrested for forcible rape which is five times greater than their proportionate representation in the nation's total population" (p. 46). In Philadelphia, according to Amir, 82 percent of 1292 rapists arrested were black.

According to the subcultural theory, lower-class black culture carries norms relevant to violent behavior, including forceful sexual exploitation. Members of the subculture are segregated and pushed into ghettos, where they learn norms and traditions primarily from other subculture members. "Differential association"—enforced by racial prejudice—works to maintain the culture's values more so than in the white lower class. Lower class black culture is less watered down by white, middle-class (nonviolent) influences. The subcultural theory denies any "genetic specificity" or "biological proclivity" tending toward violence. Rather, aggression is an outcome of "learned responses and social conditions contributing to criminality" (Wolfgang and Ferracuti, 1968, p. 264). Black prisoners, to a greater degree than other prisoners, come from backgrounds where they learn values supporting and undergo experiences motivating aggression.

Cool, hard, and hip, white and Latin prison sexual aggressors resemble young ghetto blacks. In the way they walk and talk, they indicate shared subcultural norms. Many of these mannerisms were acquired living in coterminous neighborhoods, or in training schools. Unlike other prisoners of their race, they often run with black cliques and sometimes form close associations with blacks they have met in other institutions. Prison sexual aggression comes from a lower-class, black-dominated subculture. When whites and Latins are sufficiently close to the subculture, they, too, can become members of it.

Given the fact that most prison rape seems to involve black aggressors and white victims, it should not surprise us that some claim that blacks rape whites for revenge. Irwin (1971), for example, holds resentment of middle-class whites by lower-class blacks to be the main cause for the black-aggressor–white-victim pattern. Scacco (1975) strongly upholds this explanation, and reports aggressors telling him they attacked their victims to get back at whites. Davis (1968a,b) cites the brutality in incidents he examined as evidence of race hatred motivating the activity.

Beyond the existence of the victim–aggressor race pattern itself, however, we encountered little empirical evidence to support this position. Neither aggressors nor their peers emphasized racial antagonism in interviews. This idea also fails to explain the significant number of blacks becoming targets and victims of aggressors. We should also consider that most rape victims of black aggressors in the street are black. If sexual aggression were primarily motivated by racial animosity, we would expect to find the same victim–aggressor ethnic pattern on the street as we find in prison.

History of Violent Behavior

Amir (1971) states, "The clue for the explanation of forcible rape may be sought in the tendency toward violent behavior of which rape is only one aspect" (p. 116). Our research applies this assertion to prison sexual aggressors. In regard to their commitment offenses, for example, 84 percent were doing time for a crime in which force or threat was used against a victim. Aggressors participated in a variety of violent crimes ranging from robbery and rape to homocide and assault. We are prevented, however, from saying that commission of a violent offense reliably predicts sexual aggression in prison: Nearly the same percentage of force used against victims occurs in the aggressor group as in the control group.

A significant difference stands out when we examine the violent disciplinary infractions of the two groups. Aggressors accumulated an average of five times more "tickets" for fighting than did the comparison group. Prison behavior may be an indication that aggressors have more violent dispositions than other prisoners, even other violent offenders. The many violent encounters found in these social histories places such men squarely in the subculture of violence.

The street crimes of aggressors parallel their sexual behavior in prison. Exploiting weak prisoners becomes part of long-range patterns of predatory violence. More aggressors in our study have been convicted of robbery than of any other offense. While these robberies are vicious, many are juvenile in intent and in execution. They are the petty preying behavior of unsophisticated youths, who take advantage of the opportunities for crime directly around them. The crimes are simple and direct, calling for little skill. They generally occur in or near the areas where the offenders live. These robberies are serious crimes primarily because force is used against the victims; potential or actual gains are pitifully small. Similar to sexual incidents we have examined where aggressors use physical force or threats, the usual pattern is for an aggressor to attempt to gain what he wants by causing the victim to fear for his safety. For example:

CA-28: Two weeks after release, robbed man at knifepoint of wristwatch, jacket, gloves, and sneakers in apartment building hallway.

CA-10: Robbed man; alleyway; armed with gun and knife.

CA-11: Robbed proprietor of newstand; night; armed with knife.

CA-20: Robbed cab driver; taxi in parking lot; night; armed with knife.

Examing these robberies, we see aggressors beginning encounters with the odds heavily in their favor. Indeed, the way some of these crimes are executed makes one wonder how they can be seen as demonstrations of "toughness" or "masculinity," as subcultural norms are presumed to interpret them. Aggressors, frequently accompanied by accomplices, generally chose victims weaker than themselves. They then confront these victims with weapons. While this sort of behavior may be effective exploitation, it seems to demonstrate little daring and courage, outside of the threat of getting caught by police. The way aggressors select victims in the street clearly parallels the way they select weaker inmates in prison. For example:

CA-1: In 1970 he and five others robbed a woman of a pocketbook and kicked her downstairs. In 1971, accompanied by an accomplice, robbed a young boy on the subway: "stomped on his feet, ruffled his hair, and punched him about the face, fracturing his nose and causing his hospitalization."

CA-15: Snatched purses; robbed elderly woman of pocketbook during course of burglary.

CA-9: With two accomplices, forcibly entered apartment; day; assaulted and robbed elderly female occupant. He and accomplice, at gunpoint, robbed a woman of her pocketbook.

CA-27: While on work release, stabbed and robbed woman in subway; night; with knife. Came up from behind and put his hand over her mouth. Took her wallet "in a very hostile and aggressive manner."

The subcultural interpretation of sexual aggression views sexual exploitation as only one part of general patterns of violence. In order for this theory to apply to our data, we must find aggressors who have carried out acts in the past indicating violent dispositions. The crimes we have been describing meet this description and substantiate the hypothesis. Not only are the crimes generally similar to each other, but in specific details they suggest a carry-over of former criminal behavior into prison life. We see this clearly, for example, in the way some aggressors choose weak victims. Prison sexual incidents may also resemble aggressor's criminal incidents in the immediate physical contact the aggressors have with such victims. Most of us have inhibitions against using "natural" weapons such as our arms and hands. While we may operate sophisticated weaponry, we recoil at the thought of holding knives to the throats of other men. Aggressors, on the other hand, seem to lack such inhibitions. Some robberies thus feature the same kind of direct physical force we see "gorillas" employing in prison:

CA-19: Attempted to rob grocery store; day. Grabbed both of the proprietors about the shoulders and neck and told them to give up their money.

AA-9: Killed victim by strangulation and stole cash.

CA-33: Severely assaulted and robbed another student while in high school. Student was hospitalized as a result.

Contrary to the case for robbery, few aggressors had previously been convicted of rape. Nearly the same percentage of aggressors were serving time for heterosexual rape as other men in the prison population (perhaps 12 percent). Aggressors' rape of women follows patterns we would expect to find among members of the subculture of violence. It has, on the face of it, little to do with sexual or psychological disorders. For example, we have several cases of gang rape by adolescents. Amir sees this type of rape as one of the purest examples of subculture sexual aggression. Motivated by group processes as much as by individual needs, it reflects a youthful, peer-dominated society. These events are part of the cultural life of the group. For example:

CA-31: Gang rape of 16-year-old girl; night; armed with knife.

CA-16: Accused of acting with two others to rape a 14-year-old girl in a clubhouse at night; also assaulted and threatened complainant with a whip in an effort to compel her not to testify against them.

Burgess and Holmstrom (1974) label another type of rape committed by aggressors the "impulse rape." This generally accompanies another crime, such as robbery, where rapists take advantage of the control they have gained over victims. Impulse rapists fit best into a subculture interpretation because the theory predicts rapists will have engaged in a wide range of activities employing violence to achieve goals. The following are examples of impulse rapists in our aggressors' files:

AA-1: Entered apartment and attacked woman; night. Attempted to rape under threat of knife; choked her and caused her to fall downstairs.

AA-11: Armed with knife, stole traveler's checks and cash from woman and forced her to submit to sexual contact; day.

AA-14: Assaulted, robbed, raped, and committed anal sodomy on woman; armed with knife.

Three aggressors in our sample were doing time for raping adult or adolescent males on the street. In prison, they simply continued their preprison careers. These men are few in number, and the crime they are convicted of is rare. We would not expect to find three such offenders in any other group of 45 inmates. The existence of the category shows that there may be some connection between male sexual aggression in prison and the rare crime of homosexual rape in the street. These men, unlike most aggressors, are sexual deviates, though they still came from the subculture of violence. Their backgrounds enabled them to employ force in the service of abnormal sexual needs. Here is an example of such a career. (AA-7):

1962 — Armed with knife, stole a wristwatch and 25 cents from 14 year old.

1965 — Armed with knife, forcibly engaged in acts of anal and oral sodomy with 16-year-old boy.

1972 — Assaulted young man with his fists and a cane, threatened him with a pistol, stole $37, and forcibly attempted to commit an act of sexual intercourse.

1973 — Beat boy, 13 years of age, demanded he remove his clothing, and attempted to perpetrate an act of deviant sexual intercourse on him.

Social History

Only 5 percent of the aggressors finished high school and 37 percent went no further than the eighth grade. Our aggressors' failure at education places them in a social position meeting the requirements of the subcultural hypothesis, which calls for violent men to lack "legitimate" or "symbolic" expressions of masculinity. However, since low educational levels are more generally associated with offenders, aggressors differ only slightly from the comparison group. Aggressors are part of a population of men with low educational levels; failure at school may help to explain their behavior, but the factor must be seen operating along with other variables.

We found significant differences in occupation between the aggressor and comparison groups. Most aggressors (82 percent) are in the "no occupation or student" category. As in Amir's study, most of our aggressors, in the street, depended on their families for support. Young and jobless, they have little or no work experience, and get by on petty thievery or meager handouts from welfare mothers. They share social and economic conditions common to the majority of young violent offenders in our society.

Data on family background tend to support the subcultural notion, although aggressors differ little from other prisoners on this variable. As predicted by the compulsive masculinity hypothesis, most (80 percent) of the aggressors come from broken families. In most of these (71 percent), a woman was head of the household. Clearly, if it is true that sexual aggression spawns in childhood environments lacking male identity figures, aggressors' violence may be aimed toward enhancing masculinity. Our evidence consists of the fatherless home and the aggressive outcome; we have no systematic proof for any psychological mechanism linking family background to behavior. Moreover, since the proportion of men in the comparison group from fatherless homes is almost as high as the proportion of men in the aggressor group (61 percent compared to 71 percent), we can be certain that growing up in a fatherless home is not a sufficient condition for prison sexual aggression.

The Contribution of Confinement

Irwin (1971) places aggressors in a prisoner category that he calls "state-raised youths." As a result of having spent periods of adolescence in reform schools, their sexual outlook has become aggressive and predatory. In confinement, these state-raised youths have learned to view other males as acceptable sex objects. Similarly, Jack L. Ward (1958) observes that in training schools "bullying and aggressive homosexual behavior become confused with manliness, while dependence and submission are involved with passive homosexual behavior" (p. 306).

We have some evidence for Irwin's hypothesis. Fifty-three percent of our aggressors spent time in a juvenile institution as compared to 29 percent of the comparison group—a statistically significant difference. This association alone, however, is scant proof that adult aggressors learn the behavior in juvenile institutions. Nonetheless, while the few whites in our sample must make us cautious in generalizing, it is interesting to note that four out of six white aggressors experienced juvenile commitment, as compared to 20 out of 39 blacks. This finding tends to confirm our statement that whites often become socialized to the ways of aggressors in training schools, where they are in contact with incarcerated delinquents. This may be slight evidence that the training schools affect future sexual behavior, but we also must take into consideration the probability of boys being sent to training schools because they are generally more aggressive than other boys.

Another explanation sees aggressors as long-timers—men forced by long confinement into depravity. Our data disprove this notion. More aggressors were serving shorter sentences than inmates in the comparison group. Few aggressors were serving life. Few were even serving more than four years as maximum sentences. Because these prisoners are young and their crimes are petty (though violent), aggressors avoid the lengthy sentences given to older, more sophisticated recidivists. Not only were many serving relatively short sentences, but many had only been in prison a short time before the aggressive event. For at least half of the group, this was their first term in prison. Clues such as these tend to support the view that confinement per se contributes to sexual aggression but does not serve entirely to explain it.

IS VIOLENCE AN END IN ITSELF?

Some writers, such as Davis (1968a,b) and Scacco (1975), speculating about underlying motives, claim prison aggressors abuse targets "in order to show power or dominance over other human beings" (Scacco, 1975, p. 60). When socioeconomic position blocks legitimate expressions of masculine dominance, according to this idea, violence becomes an acceptable alternative.

The idea that violence is an end in itself has little direct supporting evidence in my study. Aggressors appear used to getting what they want through threats and physical force, and they continue these patterns of exploitation in prison. Most violence that they employ appears to be either instrumental (i.e., it is used for subduing or intimidating targets) or situational (i.e., it comes from forces in the interaction itself). We know aggressors use violence when victims resist. We have seen that aggressors who threaten victims often escalate to physical force when threats do not work. We also have shown that aggressors react violently when they feel snubbed or rejected. But we have no proof for the claim that violence itself is the aggressor's primary motive. Only further research, based on in-depth interviews with aggressors, can prove or disprove this theory.

SUBCULTURAL HYPOTHESIS

When we look at aggressors alone, without comparing them to the random group, data clearly support a subcultural interpretation of prison sexual aggression. For all variables that help to confirm the theory, aggressors demonstrate relatively high percentages. Our explanation weakens, however, when we compare aggressors to the random comparison group of prisoners. Significant associations do confirm the hypothesis on some variables, such as age, ethnicity, hometown population, commitment county, violent disciplinary infractions, juvenile commitments, and occupation. Other variables, however, show only slight percentage differences when aggressors are compared to other prisoners.

The similarity of sexual aggressors to other prisoners with violent convictions weakens the strength of our conclusions. With this reservation, our data help to explain aggressors' behavior by reference to their background characteristics. However, we obviously lack ability to predict with much certainty exactly which violent black prisoners will be sexually aggressive in confinement. We know that young men, entering prison with well-established patterns of forceful exploitation, are propelled toward sexual aggression by social factors believed to govern violence. Sharing norms and values common to their subcultural peer group, they pressure targets in prison with the same style they have previously pressured others in the street (although not generally for sex). Prison sexual aggressors thus appear to continue in confinement cultural patterns learned in their communities. Subcultural membership, in the setting I examined, seems to be, in most cases, a necessary condition for sexual aggression.

Unfortunately, my analysis fails to explain why only certain prisoners with the prerequisite backgrounds become aggressors. In other words, while I establish some necessary conditions for prison sexual aggressors (i.e., factors which must be present for the event to occur), I say little about sufficient conditions (i.e., factors that in all cases lead to sexual aggression). Based on the data I presented, we cannot predict an aggressor. What are those factors that join with subcultural influences to produce acts of sexual aggression? What distinguishes a nonsexually aggressive member of this youthful subculture of violence from sexual aggressors? Is it lack of opportunity? Fear of getting caught? Resistance to group pressure? What individual psychological differences operate within a subculture of violence to control the behavior of some while others run wild? My research fails to answer these questions. I recommend them for further research.

To obtain more clues for an explanation, we must look closely at aggressors' behavior and attitudes. While our interviews fail to provide us with material for rigorous scientific inquiry, they help us to explore this area.

TYPOLOGY OF APPROACHES

From targets' descriptions I derived a tentative typology of aggressor approaches, classifying the modus operandi used by the aggressor in each incident as he approaches his victim.

Gorilla

The gorilla category is made up of tactics that rely exclusively on force or threats. "Gorillas," also known as "booty bandits," "asshole bandits," or simply "bandits," are prisoners who pounce on other men and forcibly attempt to sodomize them. In this category attempts to seduce or proposition are absent. The gorilla often takes care to set up his target. He tries to trick him to go where he can be attacked. We classified 35 percent of all approaches in the gorilla category.

AU-4: I went to the rec and this guy says, "Hey, man, a friend of mine want to talk to you." So I didn't think nothing of it. I looked around and I didn't see nobody else so I just said, "Okay." You know, I was kind of dumb to even go for it.
So then, he said, "Sneak through the door and go around. He is on the other side, waiting for you. He wants to talk to you—he has found something out for you."
I was trying to find out a way to get some smoke in. I figured I knew what he was talking about. So I got to the door and two dudes jumped out of back of the door and one of them took and put his arm around my chest and put a knife up to me—a shank—a big long shank. And there was three dudes down the other end and there was a dude standing by the cell door—all black—all six of them. It was all set up. They threw me into the cell and ripped my clothes off of me and everyone of them took me off.

*   *   *

CR-28: I was cleaning the shower and this big black guy came in and grabbed me by the throat and said, "I want some of your ass, and if you don't give it to me I am going to kill you."

*   *   *

C2-43: When I was talking to a dude, a colored dude came up behind me and yanked me and got me into a hold. He took me and dragged me down to another dude's cell and the guy was reaching his hand out and feeling my ass and stuff, I couldn't move.

Player

If we consider that aggression may be learned behavior, it is worthwhile to examine general descriptions of the culture providing such learning. Davis and Dollard, in *Children of Bondage* (1964), portray case studies of an adolescent subculture of violence in the deep South. Harold Finestone (1957), referring to Chicago slum life, writes about the "cat"—the young, lower-class black who directs his life around the search for "kicks." Perverse sex and drugs are often the tangible goals of the cat's adventures. Sexual values, according to Finestone, include aspiring to be a pimp. In *Pimp: The Story of My Life* by Iceberg Slim (1967), pimp values are more fully described through flights of exploitative fantasy. Sweet Jones, for example, the pimp in Slim's book, giving advice to a young man just starting out in his pimping career, tells him how to get his woman to work: "Make that bitch get otta that bed and get in the street. Put your foot in her ass hard. If that don't work, take a wire coat hanger and twist it into a whip" (p. 235). The pimp role includes ways of regarding women and ways of regarding violence that form a cultural backdrop to prison sexual aggression.

The player approach, comprising 29 percent of our incidents, combines force and threats with verbal tactics. Like the pimp on the street, the player aspires to fill his needs by smooth talk. Threats or physical force, however, are always ready in the background. Violence supplements, not replaces, the ensnaring rap. In the words of a prison player:

C2-51: So you run up on the dude and say, "Well, yeah, I just heard from so and so that you gave it up on Rikers Island, Man."
"What you talking about, Man?"
"I heard you did this."
"What you think I am?"
"Come on, Man, come and be my kid."
He say, "No, Man."
So you make your voice softer and you say, "I will make sure nobody messes with you. *Nobody* gonna mess with you. C'mon, man, dudes around here tell me you been taking dicks up your ass, man. I will make sure nobody mess with you. You be my kid, if you need anything, sure, man, just ask for it." And you start with that pimp line, shooting sweet melodies under his belt, "Oh, man, you are a pretty thing."
But, like when you go up on a person and ask him if he was a squeeze in a certain place and he tries to deny it—then you bring a tool along and you say, "C'mon, Man, if you deny it I am going to beat the shit out of you." Then you put a little fear into them.

The player, striving to equal the big-city pimp, imitates an ideal type, a paradigm residing in the culture from which he derives. Players thus illustrate the continuity between prison sexual aggression and normative subcultural styles prevalent on the street. Like pimps, who work at "turning out" women into money-making whores, players spend much time trying to convince targets to be their "kids." Life, for the player, centers around this homosexual hustle: It becomes a way of life, a source of satisfaction, and, perhaps, of psychological survival.

As we know from our study, many targets of players are straight. Yet the player's ideal mate is one of the highly valued prison queens. In the aggressor peer group, conquering queens gives status. And trying to conquer queens, like running games on naïve white targets, gives adventure and purpose to life. A black inmate from New York City describes players:

CR-14: These dudes read these Iceberg Slim books and walk around and put themselves on a pedestal and say they know this and that about pimping. As far as the homosexuals go, they like to be playing and be up to no good. So all they do is talk about the jailhouse bitches in the yard.

When players pursue targets who are not queens, they generally place female (or homosexual) labels on these men. A man, they reason, who looks effeminate and weak, must be "squeeze." Even if he denies it, he must have "given it up" before. Earlier we have seen how this approach upsets targets who know themselves to be heterosexual. For the player to operate his game, however, he must "feminize" his object of interest. We must remember that prisoners consider queens to be women, not men. As a consequence, the one who dominates the queen is a "man." Players live according to norms that place men who play female roles in submissive positions. One of their aims is to place naïve new prisoners in such positions, i.e., to "turn them out." The happy conclusion, as the player sees it, is for the target to become a "girl" under his domination, a receptacle for his penis, and a female companion to accentuate his masculinity.

The pimp ideal calls for success to come through virtuoso displays of intelligent and self-confident talk. In prison, however, this ideal approach often breaks down. Players are used to violence (as we see by their crimes) and fall back on force and threats when their rap gets them nowhere. The player category thus includes a mixture of verbal persuasion and threats backed by physical force. According to an aggressor peer:

AR-21: One guy will say, "Well, I'm a pimp on the streets, I can rap this out of this guy and I can do this and that." And he'll try to force them on the side, which doesn't require any fantastic game from anybody. And once the guy gives in, then he runs back and says, "Yeah, I used all this, I was into Freud and this and that."

Propositioning Approaches

About a third of the aggressors' approaches are simply nonviolent requests for sex or "propositions." No threats or force are deployed. Some of these approaches are made by gorillas and players who fear authorities or who mean to move in later with force or threats. Targets, reacting to propositions with violence, stop short some of these exploiting sequences. Other propositioning approaches, however, are considerate and ethical probes that are aimed toward mutually consenting homosexuality. But men may be approached politely for sex and still perceive themselves to be threatened. Target perceptions, in such cases, create aggressors. The propositioning category is an important one. The absence of blatant threats or force can still leave the approach a threatening one:

ARE-2 He got started in the E Block. And he said that somebody had told him my name. And then, anywhere I went, he would go. And he said, "I'm just curious. I'm just watching." And he said, "If I find out that you are homosexual then I'm going to hurt you for lying." And the dude told me once, "Hey, you're not gay, right? If I find out that you are then I'm going to kill you for not participating with me." So now he just watches me. He inquires about what I'm doing. And I tell him it's none of his business. And he sends me crazy letters.

*   *   *

C2-6: The first night that I was there two tier boys came down to my cell and said that the practice while you were in prison was to go with a homosexual, do things for other people and then other people would do things back for you. And I told him that I couldn't be part of the system. So he said, "You're in trouble now."

It is difficult to generalize about the motives and the intentions of men carrying out propositioning approaches. The category contains a mixture of men and, like the other categories, classifies bits of behavior rather than people. Certainly, some men who carry out propositioning approaches are benign persons looking desperately for warmth and sexual stimulation. But even such men, when obsessed, may be traumatizing.

GROUP PROCESS

Sexual aggression in the free world is commonly a group activity. In Amir's (1971) study, for example, 43 percent of the females were victims of multiple aggressors. Drawing on the extensive literature about gang behavior, Amir sees group rape as one form of violent gang activity. The gang has values supporting the activity. Females are defined as sex objects. Rape is viewed favorably, even enhancing or establishing masculine "rep" (Kanin, 1967). Given this favorable value climate, group processes reduce inhibitions and neutralize guilt, so that "contagion" takes over (Redl, 1949). Relevant emotion spreads from one youth to another much as though they were all breaking windows in a rampage of vandalism. The leader's behavior bolsters the courage of the followers and the presence of the followers may in turn be the stimulus for the leader to begin the activity (Amir, 1971). Geis (1971) points out the importance in such groups of members sustaining an image for the benefit of their fellows. These roles are played to the detriment of victims, for group rape often calls for even more violence than individual rape (Amir, 1971). Some suggest this to be so because in sharing the same sexual outlet group members open themselves to accusations of homosexuality— accusations that can be repudiated by treating the victim roughly (Amir, 1971).

When a group acts, causal explanations for individual behavior need not extend to everyone in the group. Blanchard (1959), who studied two group rapes, found the leader alone to be a violent offender, a man who differed from his followers in possessing "clearly defined sadistic impulses." Amir points out that when a group rape is preceded by intimidation with a weapon, it is generally the leader who wields the weapon. Struck by the difference between leaders and followers in group rape, he divides group rapists into "core members," "reluctant participants," and "nonparticipants." We must be careful in deducing general theories about aggressive motivation from the tabulated characteristics of rapists. As Geis (1971) points out, group processes in youthful gangs may be so strong as to submerge the influence of individual characteristics. The subcultural man, with the necessary background conditions to carry out sexual violence, may be propelled by excessive susceptibility to group codes and group intoxication. Similarly, a prisoner with these necessary background conditions may be inhibited from acting sexually aggressive because his drives toward group allegiance are weak.

Similar to rape on the street, much of prison sexual aggression comes from aggressors acting together: Multiple aggressors carried out 44 percent of the incidents we studied. Aggressor gangs are most common in gorilla attacks and forceful player approaches. Aggressors' friends look out for guards, set up targets, or hold down victims. Acting to please peers, caught up in the excitement of a common adventure, prison aggressors can be explained, in part, by group psychology. Examining aggressors' crimes reinforces this view, for in the street, as in prison, aggressors often carry out violent exploitation in groups.

Only some prisoners join sex gangs; most avoid them. But some men, seeking group acceptance, may be required to participate. Similarly, for men of the same type, drug use, gang fighting, or stealing may have been mandatory for membership in some cliques in the street. Differential responses to group pressure help to explain why only certain men with backgrounds required by the subcultural hypothesis become aggressors. Members of the aggressors' subculture describe peer processes leading to sexual aggression:

AR-12: And then you have got the type of dude, he don't do nothing—work every day—maybe don't participate in no sports—don't do nothing. The dude may come up to him and say, "Come on, man, let's drink some wine."

He will say, "No, I don't drink."

"Come on, let's smoke weed."

"I don't smoke weed."

And the next thing you know they will say, "He is a square—don't fuck with him. He is a chump. He don't come down with us."

And then you have got another type of dude that wants to be down with everything. He wants to hang out. He wants to be the showboat. He wants to be everything. So he is automatically accepted. He can play any role. He can play the role of the bandit and be accepted.

* * *

AR-6: It is like a gang thing. If one guy sees a homie—"Hey, so and so and so" well, see, already he just commits himself right there because from that point on he is going to go right into that road where his friends is at.

* * *

AR-5: Let's say that you have a bunch of friends and they get to talking about it was good and the person that they had the sex with. And if they are constantly talking about this, you don't have anything in common if you haven't done it. So what do you do—you do it. So that you can have something to relate with.

Within the community of prisoners, gorillas and rough players live somewhat apart. They are feared by targets and scorned by ethical prisoners. They repel men who want to stay out of trouble. Just as prison security protects weak inmates by controlling sexual aggressors, targets are protected by the fact that most prisoners are concerned about getting out. Men need good behavior records to keep good time, to get parole, and to avoid additional criminal charges. Many, thus, for logical reasons, avoid joining aggressor cliques. In addition to such external controls, men avoid the activity because they believe it is wrong. Prisoners we interviewed put down aggressors who use force, describing them as deviants and fringe members of society. It is only the immediate members of the gorilla gangs who provide a supportive group climate for the behavior:

AR-12: The first thing you probably hear is, "Stay away from him. He is a bandit." This follows the person any place he goes. Any institution he goes to there is always going to be someone that knows him from another institution, you know, and every time you walk out in the yard or something, someone is going to point at him and say, "See, that guy there—stay away from him and watch him—he is a bandit."

Less physically abusive aggressors may be accepted by other inmates. The player who wins a target through intelligent rap may be admired for his resemblance to the successful pimp. Still other aggressors may not be seen as aggressors by anyone but their targets. These men are not put down by others because they are seen as respectable and ethical men who cope with long-term sex deprivation by seeking consensual affairs. A long-timer tells us:

AR-12: Just because you are locked up, that doesn't mean you haven't got no morals. But like the fellows in the institution, they don't frown upon it. The only way they frown upon the dude is if the dude that takes them off really roughs them up. Like a young kid might come in and he just go and beat him up, and take something from him. Then everybody frowns upon that.

A Group Rape

The following narrative by a participant brings out group themes in sexual aggression. The incident takes place on the adolescent side of the Jamesville penitentiary in Onondaga County, New York. The aggressors are urban blacks, convicted prisoners serving sentences. The victim is an American Indian:

AR-12: Say, like, one time, a couple of guys wanted to rip a kid off, and both of them was smaller than I was. They could see that I was down with that crowd so they just used me and they said, "Well, we are going to go into the guy's cell and you just come in there with us." It was just a spur of the moment thing; we was all just like children. We never really planned anything. We might be sitting around and talking. Like the idea would hit one of us and we would say it to the rest. Then everybody would go along and that is what we did. . . .

    Well, see, what you have is a long gallery and now the officer sits at the end of the gallery at a desk. It is behind a wall. If he happens to have to get up and look around the gallery, he can see what is going on. But the officer, he don't care. He is an old guy and he is reading his books and paper and what not. He was at his desk, just sitting there, and me, Bill, and another friend of mine go into the empty cell—like, all the cells are open.

    This is about mid day. And Audie stands out there in front of the cell and he calls the guy. And so the guy comes down to see what he wants. This other dude and I snatch the dude right into the cell and then they start telling him to undress. He sees me there and, like, you know, he can get scared, right? And I am not saying nothing to him, I am trying to put myself in the position, like—if he decides to go to the police and tell them what is happening, if he tells the truth, he can't say that I did anything to him, and I don't put my hands on him—So the guy sees me there and so he starts getting scared. What they did was use my presence to get what they wanted from the kid. Getting directly involved, I don't think that I could handle five or six years for something like that. . . .

He just undressed. I guess that he feared that he would get beat up for not having sex with another man. And so after they have sex with him they unlock the cell. He didn't tell. He just tried to stay away from everybody as much as possible. And he left and he came back and he didn't stay very long, only about two days because when he came back the second time his mother died or something and he had to go to a funeral so he went out and didn't come back. . . .

He was only 17, right, but like he seemed to me to be a lot younger than that. He acted a lot younger than that. He was quite naïve and it seemed like it might have been his first time to come into jail. And he didn't know anything about how to do this and how to do that. He was just what I call him, a kid. Not that I was that old at the time, but I matured a lot quicker than a lot of dudes my age, and I was ahead of these dudes. I would suspect that he didn't bring it on himself—but he was more physically attractive than anyone else would appear at that time, because, like, it takes something to motivate that type of action, you know, and the way a dude looks has a lot to do with it. If you come in and you look like a girl, well, sure, they are going to want to have something to do with you.

He was a kid, but, like, he wasn't small by any means. He was mild like and he was heavy but he wasn't built strongly. He was tall and kind of heavy but you could look at him and tell that he was soft because a lot of times we would be out playing basketball and quite a few times he played with me and I told him, "Look, don't let the man just shoot the ball like that." And the guy would just run right over him just like that—and he was just weak.

The example summarizes many of the ideas that are discussed here. Easily influenced by peers, this aggressor looks upon an assault as a kick—a spontaneous adventure. Similar to some heterosexual rape, the group is marked by different degrees of involvement. We even see specialization, as the group members use different abilities to set the victim up and intimidate him. The victim is chosen because of his perceived weakness and his physical attractiveness. Interestingly, the informant choses the victim's performance in a basketball game to describe attributes contributing to his perceived weakness: the victim lets other players "run right over him." The aggressors know that the victim is an easy mark because he fails their test of masculine strength—assertiveness and physical aggression. In this incident, aggressors have the necessary background characteristics, the necessary group formation, and a stereotypical target. The guard, on the gallery but inattentive, allows these factors to lead to a concrete event. His laxity, along with the aggressor and target characteristics, explain the rape.

AGGRESSOR SEXUALITY

Male and Female Roles

Aggressors, men with long-term heterosexual orientations, desire women. Along with some men in the random group, they tell us that after a certain period of time they begin to view certain male prisoners as desirable females. Targets, they tell us, arouse sexual desire.

AR-18: Some men look feminine and looks are enough alone for a man behind these walls to attempt to try and get him. It is a hell of a thing to say, but here you are another man and you are behind these walls and before long another man begins to look like a woman to you.

*   *   *

CA-2: We have these young ones and they have still got baby skin and long hair, you know, and they resemble a woman as close as they can get it. The whites, among the younger generation, have got long hair, they have still got baby skin, they are soft, you know—like women. They resemble a woman and you just start to watch. Some of them have feminine ways. You begin to watch those with feminine ways. They don't have homosexuality within them, but still they have feminine ways. You watch them just to take your mind off women. And there ain't nothing you can do about it.

Virtually all observers of prison find that aggressors consider themselves to be masculine and that they view their targets as substitute women. Clemmer's (1958) typology, not explicitly concerned with sexual aggression, has been continually employed to explain these sex roles: "wolves," "jockers," and "daddies" play masculine roles;

"punks" play female roles. Seeing targets as female, aggressors conceive themselves to be male and heterosexual. In sexual terms, this translates into the "man" being the active partner in the relationship (i.e., he inserts his penis into the mouth or anus of the prisoner in the female role). A sophisticated target tells us how he confronted an aggressor by questioning this premise:

C2-15: I was sitting down at a table and playing poker with this guy. Some guy comes up to me and taps me on the shoulder and says, "I am going to fuck you in your ass." So I just turned to him and I said, "What are you, some kind of faggot?" He said, "Well, if I fuck you in the ass, you are the punk and you are the faggot and I am the man for being able to do it." So I asked him if he knew the meaning of a homosexual. He said, "No." And so I usually have my poem book—I always carry a dictionary—and I pulled it out and I looked up homosexual and I said to him, "Read that." He read it and he said, "That don't mean nothing."

Aggressors, along with other members of their group, view passive (or "insertee") sexual behavior as shameful. An associate of two aggressors reported that he caused his friends to desist from trying to rape another prisoner by first asking, "How would you feel if someone rolled on you and did that? You would feel very ashamed." He then pointed out to his friends what might happen if the authorities caught them gang-raping a fellow prisoner and communicated the fact to their mothers: "We don't want these people writing home and saying that you got caught in sexual acts, see, because it doesn't tell who is doing who."

By any definition relative to self-concept, the prison sexual aggressor is heterosexual. He prefers women, placing men in female roles. The folder of an inmate aggressor confirms this fact with an interesting bit of personality diagnosis:

Counselor's Report: It was reported that Jones had been making alleged homosexual advances toward another inmate employee of the Mess Hall. Mr. Line referred Jones to the Mental Health Unit for evaluation to determine the possible need for therapy. Jones was subsequently administered an intelligence test and the Minnesota Multiphasic Personality Inventory by Mr. Smith. Mr. Smith reported that although this individual's personality characteristics showed immaturity, hostility, rebelliousness, poor standards and impulsiveness, that he could not be considered a homosexual.

Sexual Deprivation

What does prison literature say about the relation between sexual aggression and sexual deprivation? In spite of the fact that prison keeps heterosexual men from female contact, and in spite of the lack of evidence about the consequences of this fact, most writers do not give much weight to sexual deprivation as a cause for sexual aggression. Gagnon and Simon (1973) go so far as to claim prisoners do not even have strong sexual urges while incarcerated; Davis (1968a,b) and Buffum (1972), whose writings are widely quoted, adopt the same position.

While no systematic evidence supports either side of the question, some observers close to the prison claim that sexual deprivation is a major concern of inmates. Clemmer (1958), for one, considers "sex yearning . . . the most painful phase of incarceration" (p. 256). Bloch (1955) believes prisoners have strong sexual thoughts, which are continually reinforced by the "aphrodisiac quality of modern media" (p. 122). Writing about sexual deprivation in an Indian prison, Srivastava (1974) states that "its grip over prisoners minds is very pressing" (p. 21).

What about deprivation and aggression in the free community? E. J. Kanin (1965) carried out empirical studies on this question, using college men for informants. Kanin claims that "aggressives entertain significantly higher subjective estimates of their sex drive than do the nonaggressives" (p. 229). Reporting that aggressives, more successful at arranging sex than nonaggressives, were also more dissatisfied by their experiences, Kanin concludes that sexual deprivation, rather than being a function of absolute deprivation, depends on the disparity between erotic aspirations and erotic accomplishments. Sexual frustration, according to this idea, would be more intense for those prisoners who have been or are sexually active than for those who have been sexually quiescent. Thus, in prisons the men with the greatest sexual experience, those with the most developed "erotic aspirations," could be the most sexually frustrated and, consequently, the most aggressive. This could relate to the prevalence of aggression among blacks, for studies by Gold (1970) and Ehrmann (1964) indicate premarital sexual behavior is more widespread among black youths than white youths. Moreover, while doing time, blacks seem more likely than whites to become involved with prison queens. Consequently, Kanin's idea could help to explain why black prisoners are more sexually aggressive than white prisoners, provided that experienced deprivation is a mediating variable.

We spoke with aggressors who told us that they pursue other men because of strong sexual urges. One man, for example, who sexually assaulted a fellow prisoner two weeks before our interview, describes how it feels for him to be sexually deprived, and how that feeling (as he sees it) leads to aggressive episodes:

CA-2: Like, you have so much time to think about these things; like, you lay up in your cell for this certain time, and for a certain amount of time you get tired of reading. And you get tired of listening to the radio so all you do is think. You think about women all the time that you are in your cell. But when you come out all you see is men. So you say, "That is just the next best thing." You are not just going to push the thoughts of women out of your head, because it is impossible. You are a man and you have got to think about it—about women. . . . It gets to the point where you say, "I have just got to stop thinking about it." It seems to bug me, you know. You will be thinking about it and all, you know, like one thing leads to another. You get a letter from your girlfriend, and you think about all the other girls. And then it starts to build up until your head is filled with thoughts, but all you see around you is men, men, men. So you just say, I have got to get . . . I am going to start messing with the homos. I am going to start messing with the queens.

Aggressors who spoke openly about their behavior sometimes expressed guilt and remorse over having been driven to such lengths. On the other hand, they saw a preemptory sex drive behind their activities, and blamed the prison and other external forces for creating the pressing problem that inevitably forced their actions:

CA-2: Everybody is after somebody, but it all boils down to the same thing: they want sex—they want sex. You get to the point that you don't care no more and you get it from them. I feel, like, it is just something crazy to be attacking another man or trying to take his manhood from him when you wouldn't want yours taken from you. You come here as a whole—you should go home as a whole. But it is something that certain people get to the point where they can't avoid this no more. You get to a point where you just don't care no more. How can you cope with being sexually deprived for three years, for two, for even five years at a time?

* * *

CA-19: It makes you into a sick person. It turns you into a sick person. Like, you are crazy over men—you want men. You go on the side with the men and things like this. You crave over men, and you go in your cell and you masturbate about three or four times a day. And then you look at men. It really turns you into an animal. When you go into prison, and then you go out with your people, you don't even know how to act. You even look at your mother. It really turns you into an animal. Sick. They should give you something for you to control it or something.

* * *

AR-5: It is being deprived and dreaming and plotting and scheming: "What I am going to do when I have the opportunity." It makes you mean, evil, and scheming. It does terrible things to you. I am so cognizant of what it has done to me. It has affected me in more ways than I can even explain. It has taken some of the humanistic qualities which I know I would have continued to possess if I had not been deprived. It has made me callous in respects.

I can stand and watch a person being sexually assaulted and it wouldn't bother me a bit because I have seen so much of it. It wouldn't be a shock. It has done certain things to me. It has made me permissive in certain ways that I know I wouldn't have been. It just takes away some things. I guess it is a constant viewing of these things that just tears down the horror of seeing it for the first time. The first time it is, "Wow, these guys are sick." You know what I am saying? After you have been in for a while, you say, "I haven't had no sex either."

Paradoxical as it may strike us, aggressors can thus not only justify their acts but can argue that they, ultimately, are the real victims.

Prison Staff

 Probably no aspect of our topic is discussed with more accusation than the role of staff. Weiss and Friar (1975), for example, claim:

> Officials find rapists particularly useful . . . authorities frequently encourage prison rape and very rarely prevent it. . . . Most prison authorities have no intention of stopping it. . . .

Can anyone deny that sexual terror is the policy of the American prison? (p. 121)

Similarly, Scacco, author of *Rape in Prison* (1975), claims that "administrators and staff treat it [sexual aggression] as non-existent" (p. 30); they ignore inmate complaints and support victim isolation by pretending that the problem does not exist.

Work based on field research paints a less accusatory but still dismal portrait. Describing how juvenile targets get "meaningless" advice from staff, Bartollas et al. (1976) tell how staff advise scapegoats (always weak inmates) not to "let anyone push you around" (p. 59). They indicate that staff tend to blame targets for bringing victimization on themselves, e.g., by failing to fight. Toch (1975), in his study of prison breakdowns, notes how traditional job roles may discourage officers from helping men. Staff concern for custody—their primary function—results in neglecting subjective and psychological consequences of management.

STAFF UNDERSTANDING OF THE PROBLEM

We used three sources of information to assess the staff role: (1) target interviews, (2) staff reports in target files, and (3) staff interviews. After compiling this data, we were able to answer some basic questions. In the first place, we found that staff knew about two-thirds of the incidents targets described. In half of these cases, targets themselves reported the events to staff. In the others, staff observed the incident. The fact that two out of three of these aggressive episodes were known to staff tells us sexual aggression is not hidden behavior.

Staff perceptions of potential targets parallel some of our findings. A captain tells us, "Any good-looking white boy will be pressured, but small, young, country boys have it the worst." Deputy superintendents, counselors, and officers have told us the same thing. Their predictive indicators include both objective and subjective indices. The following, for example, are excerpts from inmate files:

> *Vocational Education Report:* Observed as rather meek, mild, and gullible youth that could become a "target" of the hardened and aggressive inmates if not closely supervised.

> *Attica Classification Evaluation Summary:* His physical makeup could create problems for him in population; he is very reserved and young looking.

> *Elmira Summary:* It should be noted that he looks much younger than his chronological age and does impress as one who could be easily manipulated by aggressive inmates.

> *Coxsackie Record:* Very immature, naïve, and rural type youth. Will experience some peer pressure here.

Information about inmate problems flows to staff while they carry out their varied duties. Officers, just like policemen on the street, openly observe misbehavior. More detail is added, behind closed doors, as custody administrators interview targets and aggressors, investigating possible crimes or disciplinary infractions. Mental health issues often surface when targets ask to be moved to another job, housing block, or institution. Targets may not want to share information with staff but may be forced into some revelations in order to undergird the legitimacy of transfer requests. Crisis requests thus may reveal crisis conditions.

130

Psychiatric Report: He said he is thinking quite seriously about getting a transfer because he is pressured by inmates and tired of running. He just feels that sooner or later he is going to fall victim to some man who is pursuing him.

He did state that if anyone here at Attica attempted to rape him, he would really seriously think about committing suicide. States he does not want to come to the Psychiatric Unit unless he is forced to come here.

C.O.'s Report: Started throwing his bed and furniture around . . . says he cannot take it any longer in B-1 div. . . . requests to be moved to C-2.

Staff, as part of "classification," interview newly arriving men. Here, fearful prisoners, worried targets, have an opportunity to open up to staff, providing that the interviewer can draw out the information and that the inmate is willing to talk. Classification is where prisoners are tested, evaluated, and observed; it is one of the most obvious occasions for men to inform staff about their adjustment problems. In the following "case analysis" from Elmira, we see how a sensitive "classification analyst" learns about a man's problem and makes out a "program" in response to special needs related to victimization.

[Inmate] states that individuals currently confined at Elmira Reformatory both assaulted and sodomized him while he was at Rikers Island . . . does appear to be a victim of rather harrowing experience, i.e., his problem while confined at Rikers.

The writer, with the cooperation of the company officer and Service Unit at the Reformatory, checked into the matter and there is a possibility that his claims are valid. However, there is no recording of the incident available. However, it would most likely be in his best interest . . . that he not be transferred to Elmira Correctional Facility.

He is a rather pathetic type individual and talks to a great extent about the trauma he suffered while at Rikers Island. The most important aspect of his future adjustment would appear to be placement in a secure situation where he would be able to pursue a program . . . and where his experience at Rikers Island could diminish in their influence. Therefore, what appears most important here is placing this individual in a situation where he might be able to participate in the program free from his main problem, that of fear itself.

Some staff, especially officers and work supervisors, have sufficient informal contact with prisoners to hear about problems. Such communication occurs especially between younger inmates and older officers who have established reputations for being fatherly. Disciplinary proceedings offer another key informational juncture. Aggressor and target violence bring the problem to the attention of custody administrators, who have primary responsibility for enforcing the rules governing inmate discipline. In addition to punishing prisoners, the modern prison disciplinary process is supposed to help them. Thus, in the "adjustment committee," or prison court, sometimes assistance follows disclosure of the real cause for fighting. For example:

> *Adjustment Committee Report:* Inmate admits other inmates are after him for sex and that he owes two cartons of ciggs. to inmate in DI. Recommendation: Change of program and transfer to C-2.

The line staff, who supervise prisoners directly, prepare reports for the adjustment committee. Based on their observations and their understanding of the problem, officers transmit (or neglect to send on) information. This can be seen as part of a referral system. An officer, observing a discipline problem based on sexual aggression, can, if he chooses, initiate a process possibly culminating in a troubled man being helped.

> *Misbehavior Report:* Kessler was involved in a fight with Johnson. Johnson slapped Kessler in the face. The cause of this confrontation is unknown to me. However, Kessler seems to be involved in a lot of disputes in C-2. He is a weak inmate and is easily led by the stronger inmates.

> *ERC Company Officer's Report:* He has the constant feeling that other inmates are always out to get him . . . I feel, at the transfer facility, Morrison will need guidance and counseling, and possibly close supervision.

While the mental health view looks to men who *are troubled*, the custody view handles men who *are in trouble*. In relation to target violence, for example, staff sometimes overlook or encourage fighting when it serves inmate self-defense. Another manifestation of the custodial perspective is the concern for guilt and innocence that is contained in the custodial view of sexual aggression. Important questions are: Did the prisoner invite the sexual approach? Have the aggressors committed a legally definable crime?

A concern for physical safety marks the custodial approach. Is the man in danger? If so, what can be done to guard him? While psychiatrists apply medication, custodial men must apply physical barriers and human surveillance to manage the problem. These measures, for the most part, accomplish the limited objective of providing a relatively safe environment for most men. Aggressors, as we have seen, persist in subtle behavior that is possible even within the strictest discipline; but if aggressors go too far or become too blatant, staff generally move in rapidly.

Staff are most successful, and are most diligent, in handling the types of aggressive sexual behavior defined as legal crimes. In cases of alleged rape that are known to staff, the process begins with a thorough "administrative investigation." From the law enforcement point of view, these investigations are handled professionally. The following lieutenant's report is a case in point.

On Friday afternoon, at approximately 3:00 P.M., C.O. Stuart, Block Officer, informed me that inmate Figliani #11176, an F Block worker, had been reportedly been having oral sexual relations with a number of inmates. This was reported to Stuart by another inmate. I instructed C.O. Stuart to question Figliani and let me know the results.

At approximately 3:30 P.M., as I was leaving the Adjustment Committee, C.O.s Dell and Stuart called me to F Block where they were talking to Figliani. At this time, they informed me that Figliani had told them that he had been sexually assaulted in C Block the previous night, November 21, 1974, at about 8:15 P.M. He stated that he had gone to D Block for Night Rec., with I Block, and while there was thrown into C Block by black inmates and assaulted sexually. This would have been approximately 20 hours before he reported this.

I asked him if he was bleeding or was hurt, and he stated that he did not know. I ordered Figliani placed in S.H.U. for protection and instructed the officers to obtain any further information they could.

At this time, I proceeded to my South Mess Hall assignment—time was approximately 3:40 P.M. After arriving at the South Mess Hall, I notified Lt. Hutton, Acting Captain, of the incident and my actions. I called the count desk and instructed the Sgt. to inform Lt. Williams, Tour No. 2 Lt., to arrange for Figliani to be examined medically as soon as possible and filled him in on the situation.

After the count, approximately 5:00 P.M., I stopped at the count desk and checked with Lt. Williams to be sure he was fully informed on the situation. He was, at this time, talking to R.N. Weber on the phone. Lt. Williams indicated to me that R.N. Weber had some questions concerning the situation and I asked him to let me speak to her, and I did. Because of the lapse of time between the alleged assault, R.N. Weber indicated that it would not probably be useful to examine the subject. But after further discussion, I told her we would send the inmate to the

133

hospital for an examination. I wanted it to be a matter of record that the inmate was checked medically for further evidence and for treatment, if necessary.

When sexual assaults occur, administrators generally assume that established procedures were not being followed. A door, supposed to be locked, was left open; an officer, supposed to be up and about, was taking it easy in his office; prisoners, supposed to be in one place, somehow were allowed to wander. Having enacted custody measure designed for total control (and total safety), administrators blame sexual assaults on failures to carry out these measures. However, officers and their supervisors carry on a constant guerrilla action against prisoners determined to break rules. No matter how diligent staff may be, no matter how professional, the war continues unrelentingly. While staff control prisoners most of the time, sexual assaulters, as we have seen, always manage "to score a few victories." More importantly, much aggressor activity—unless it results in fights—barely violates institutional rules. Most formal custody procedures only cover acts by gorillas (and possibly some players).

Informal as well as formal measures are taken to control aggressors. A captain in the youth prison, getting "wolves'" names from complaining targets, keeps a special list of these men. Their movements are monitored, and some jobs and housing areas are not available to them. They become informally classified as "maximum custody" and are treated with more attention than other inmates. The captain himself, when he knows of aggressors being active, calls them into his office and tells them to "lay off." This measure works, or so the captain tells us.

A variety of program staff learn about the problem. Counselors and mental health professionals have job duties that call for them to learn of, and manage, inmate difficulties. Staff in other areas sometimes depart from their formal job roles to become concerned about individual inmates, at least to the extent of putting others on notice that here is a man who needs special attention.

Physical Ed. Report: A very weak and timid acting individual who appears to be rather fearful of his surroundings.

Vocational Education Report: Mentioned he has been bothered by the usual type inmates that enjoy picking on and bulldozing this meek, defenseless type youth.

General Education Report: Claims blacks have threatened his life because of his resisting attempts at sexual activity. He has been unable to see himself surviving in this environment . . . [needs] situation that has sufficient support so that he could at least feel as nonthreatened as possible.

Crisis requests and classification interviews are especially likely to bring forth the target's mental condition. Staff, observing a man's severe reactions to fear, often make a psychiatric referral. Once a psychiatrist is brought into the picture, a formal diagnosis concerning a target's reaction to the situation is generally made. In their diagnoses, psychiatrists, learning of the target's fear, emphasize the inmate's reaction to the outward stimuli more than the stimuli itself. Consequently, the recommendations frequently include "medication," such as tranquilizers, enabling the target to cope with anxiety. The following are examples of psychiatrists' diagnoses and recommendations.

Psychiatric Report: Psychiatric episode at Elmira is, in my opinion, a dissociative reaction precipitated by the stress in incarceration. Only recently that his anxiety has subsided concerning other people hurting him.

Memo, Reception Psychiatrist to Superintendent: Most likely he seems to be a desirable person to be victimized by the other inmates. Uneasy, tense, nervous and having trouble sleeping at night. . . . Valium 10 mg. is recommended.

Psychiatrist to superintendent [referred because wanted to do entire bit in protection]: He seems to be very much concerned about the other inmates that approach him to poke him in the rear end. This idea of other people taking advantage of him seems to create a great deal of anxiety as well as tension. He says he cannot take it anymore . . . his tension and anxiety is mounting to the point he feels he is going to "flip out—go crazy—or have a nervous breakdown." At times he gets shaky, fearful, and during interview, while talking about it, he is almost on the verge of tearfulness. His eyes get red. . . .

Although his reality testing still remains intact, however, overall his defense mechanism becomes very blurry and tenuous. He is not fully psychotic at this time. However, he is a problem, requires constant supervision and support. Recommendation: Serox, 30 mg. TID; reasonable support, supervision, and observation.

A current trend, in both the youth and the adult prison, is to refer an aggressor, regardless of the level of force he has employed, to a psychiatrist. While the psychiatrist is presumably called in under the questionable assumption that the aggressor needs treatment for his "perversion," such action probably has a deterrent effect. The psychiatrist's report goes in the file, warning the aggressor that his behavior may affect both his institutional treatment and his release date. Any real treatment, however, is generally stalled by client resistance. Aggressors seldom talk openly about their actions. Even when faced with overwhelming evidence, they tend to deny their guilt, and effectively turn treatment sessions into adjudicatory trials.

When staff notice a man becoming a target, they often get other staff with whom the inmate is in contact to watch him. They may do the same for aggressors involved.

Case Analysis: During interview at the Reception Center claims he has been threatened by other inmates who are trying to get cigarettes from him and also attempted to force him into acts of sodomy. He gives the names of the two worse offenders as 12314, Bocci and 11781, Walker. Apparently, officers have been alerted and are watching them closely.

Progress Evaluation Report: Supervising personnel report that inmate is a very good worker and requires less than the average amount of supervision. However, because of his slight stature, it is feared that he may become the target of homosexual attacker. Inmate does not have any inclination in this direction. Therefore, various supervising personnel report that they keep an extra eye out in order to prevent any such situation.

Counselor's Notes: Resident came to counselor complaining about Robert Gibson, 11684, who had been making advances to him in the kitchen. Counselor called mess hall. They said, Mr. Gibson is indeed a homosexual who tends to favor younger males. . . . They keep an eye on him because of this.

Staff also arrange safe housing. An employee may be effective at cutting through red tape by making a few calls. He can talk convincingly to the right administrators, and in a short time can pull a desperate prisoner out of a dangerous setting and place him in a safe one. Sometimes a similar process takes place even before a man is threatened. In the adult prison, authorities sometimes place vulnerable inmates in protective niches. Such a niche may be, for example, a job in the officer's mess or a housing assignment offering protection from attack. Sometimes attempts are made to mask such efforts. The inmate may not even be told of the reason for the assignment. The purpose of this secrecy is to prevent the vulnerable inmate from being labeled "weak" by other convicts. Through this process, a diligent and sensitive staff can reduce the incidents of sexual aggression.

For these tactics to be effective, a vulnerable convict should be identified while he is in reception awaiting classification. This identification is an informal decision and may be subject to error. Staff may assume, for example, that all blacks can "make it" in the general population. Yet some blacks are just as vulnerable as whites. The problem is that determination to treat a man differently because of his potential for victimization is based on physical cues or characteristics. Fair skin, youth, effeminate ways, and small size are the usual standards. Staff, especially experienced line officers, have a stereotype of the "weak" inmate that is often correct, but is sometimes mistaken.

The second problem comes from the obstacles to providing protective niches to everyone who needs them. In one prison, for example, a certain job training program serves as an enclave of security for "weak" inmates. Yet, this training program has entrance requirements relevant to vocational rehabilitation—not to safety. Inmates who need the safety the area provides may not meet the criteria for admission to it. Similarly, in the same prison, custodial concerns prevent targets who are violent offenders from assignment to the "farm," a less threatening environment than the cell blocks behind the walls.

In the youth prison, we observed an institutionalized, formal way of extending safe housing to targets and potential targets: Close to 40 men are effectively separated from aggressors without limiting the access of those safeguarded to regular programs. Stigma is the only liability that is associated with residence in Weak Company; however, staff and prisoners feel that it is a low price to pay for protection. Block officers, reception staff, and others refer inmates to Weak Company. Some inmates resist the move. They do not want others to call them "homos" and are generally afraid for their reputation. On the other hand, any man who wants to get into Weak Company is admitted automatically, once his record is checked to make sure he is not an aggressor. If the population gets too large, another tier takes the overflow, and also receives special care.

We learned about various idiosyncratic approaches to the problem. In the adult prison, a psychiatric caseworker brought an aggressor she trusted, a man on her caseload, together with a target. Getting the assignment board to transfer the target to the coal gang where the aggressor worked, she aimed to change the aggressor by getting him to identify with the target's difficulties. In the meantime, the target was being schooled by the aggressor to avoid dangerous situations. In another case, a counselor quietly transferred a target to the block where the target's best friend lived.

ISSUES CONCERNING STAFF ACTION

The law enforcement approach to the victimization problem generally stops when physical safety (i.e., protection from sexual assault) is ensured. Beyond this, few custody-minded administrators recognize the condition as calling for improvement. The following exchange of memos highlights this view:

> *Counselor to Superintendent*: Resident indicated a fear for his life . . . according to him, this stems from the fact that inmates have been placing their hands on his body, spitting in his face, generally harassing him with sexual overtures as well as physical threats. After interviewing this resident, I interviewed an inmate who also is a member of B Company and he stated that many of the problems of this individual were brought about by his own actions. . . . Resident's present complaints are based on his inadequacy and manner in which he attempted to alleviate his fears on the gallery. Not in danger of severe physical harm . . . does not normally fit the criteria of one who . . . is in a protective problem. [Recommendation]: (1) Refer to psychiatrist. (2) Remove from present protective situation. The inmate should not be allowed to be placed in such a comfortable situation which only appears to reinforce his desire to remain out of population.

> *Superintendent to Counselor* [*same case*]: Please counsel the inmate that we do not have idle company and if he wants to shorten his incarceration, he must show positive participation in programs. If he is afraid of other inmates, advise him to comingle only in areas where supervision is constant.

As we have seen, the perception of aggression can be as trouble-some as aggression itself. If custody is only interested in physically tangible danger, a portion of the real problem receives no attention.

One obstacle standing in the way of improvement is the public policy placing restrictions on racial segregation, a move staff know would make fearful whites feel better. Of course, segregation occurs anyway, to a certain extent. Weak Company is a predominantly white division and, informally in the yard, there are ethnically homogeneous cliques. Prison jobs and housing areas, however, must remain integrated. Since at least in the youth prison, there are few whites to go around, the strongest whites—or the ones assumed to be the strongest—are sprinkled around the prison. Some tiers have three or four whites among 30 or 40 blacks and Puerto Ricans: Numerous targets come from this pool. Indeed, there is fairness in having, say, at least some whites working in the steamy kitchen rather than having all of them sitting as clerks under the eyes of officers; but the integration issue takes flexibility away from staff.

Another obstacle is the size and complexity of the prison organization. An individual prisoner's physical existence is directed by numerous staff members, some of whom never physically see him. When a problem is perceived by one staff member, the route may be long and twisted before anything is done about the problem by another staff member, especially for concerns viewed as not being matters of life or death or physical health. Staff who achieve solutions must often be persistent, vocal (and to other staff, obnoxious) advocates of prisoners' welfare.

As we have seen, staff, in the prisons we studied, were actively involved in handling the problem of sexual aggression. They recognized the concern and attempted to manage it. Knowing this, is it realistic to uphold generalities, such as the following by Carroll (1977)?

> It seems unlikely that the staff would pursue a vigorous policy of prevention. Guards have a strong interest in the maintenance of atomization and conflict among prisoners. As long as each prisoner "does his own time" or conditions approach a "war of all against all," there will be no effective challenge to the position and power of the custodians. It is thus in the interest of the guards to adopt a lax posture with respect to biracial sexual assaults. (p. 426)

Our research implies a different interpretation of the staff role. We have suggested that sexual aggressors often enter prison with well-defined patterns of violent behavior. No effective weapons exist in

139

the arsenal of correctional rehabilitation to change these propensities effectively (Martinson, 1976; Fishman, 1977). Prisons are crowded, and management and program needs call for inmates to intermingle. Considering that the factors that attract aggressors are always present in the population, some level of sexual aggression seems to be almost inevitable in any prison with the usual combination of inmates (potential aggressors and potential targets). The costs of custodial solutions, in terms of civil rights violations, extreme controls, and movement restrictions must be considered as part of the intervention. We now turn to this problem.

Alternatives to Prison Sexual Violence

Perhaps half of the incidents in this study featured physical violence. Of this, half came from aggressors coercing targets; the rest came from targets reacting to threats or perceived threats. Such violent reactions were instrumental for targets in the sense that they ended more incidents than any other response. After fights, targets reported that aggressors left them alone. Targets who had been violent said they moved around the prison with less fear, and that they felt better about themselves.

Most men interviewed held values supporting violent responses to sexual approaches. These prisoners saw violence as the medium for the message that one is "straight" (i.e., heterosexual), uninterested in sexual involvement, or tough—not a prospect to "get over on." Others simply said that violence was the best self-defense available to them because it unambiguously let the aggressor know the consequences of his behavior if he persisted. In prison, target violence usually leads to an improved self-image and a more favorable status among other prisoners. Fellow inmates, sought for guidance, advise new inmates to accept this solution. The staff support target violence and back up their counsel with a flexible disciplinary process, exempting some inmates from punishment when they fight to uphold their manhood.

Anger and irritation are emotions complementing these values. As we have seen, anger is characteristic of the target emotional response and the irritation caused by aggressors can itself lead to targets exploding in unscheduled and uncalculated ways. As in animal behavior, we see a link here between fear, anger, and aggression. Threatened men, angered men, and fearful men can easily become aggressive themselves. They then may turn exploiters into victims of violence.

Aggressors, of course, initiate as much violence as targets. We trace this "exploitative violence" to cultural patterns learned on the street in "subcultures of violence." Part of the psychological impact on targets relates to their confronting, often for the first time in their lives, these unfamiliarly high levels of violent behavior. In facing aggressors with their implications of violence, the targets perceive themselves to be in danger: Feeling that they may be raped or killed, they experience stress reactions caused by fear.

If prisons are supposed to treat criminality, the socialization of men into upholding violence defeats such an aim. If prisons are to punish fairly, their punishment falls unequally and unfairly when some offenders enjoy exploitation. If prisons are presumed to incapacitate, the goal is mocked by criminal violence thriving behind the walls. Yet prison staff can only do so much. Part of the problem of violence (target reactions) appears to be an adaptation to prison life, a way of coping with possible victimization. Another type of violence (aggressors' exploitation) reaches back into the social history of a group that makes up the prison population and is reinforced in prison. Until subcultural violence is eliminated, an unlikely prospect at this time, sexual violence will persist in prison.

IMPACT ON TARGETS

An implication of this book is that the impact of victimization is not necessarily related to the level of force deployed in an incident or to the "objective" danger of the environment. Players, pimps, and propositioners, as we have seen, often got nowhere with their approaches. Custodial staff and single cells protected almost all men from gorillas. Most targets, even by the most inept actions, avoided being pushed into homosexual activity. Threats seemed to bring compliance only in rare situations when security was inadequate and targets were cornered and overwhelmed by physical force. Yet, targets still reacted to threats and propositions as though they could easily be victims. To an extent, the impact of target experience is based on the perception of danger and the expectation of physical harm rather than actual danger and physical harm. Environments themselves, if viewed as threatening, can be responsible for victim trauma.

Concern for reducing violence related to target reactions could thus focus upon increasing targets' confidence in being able to handle situations without the drastic measures currently employed. If, indeed, most aggressors fail to achieve sexual aims, yet targets think that there is a likely chance of their being victims, then violent target reactions—coming from fear—are based on misreading the situation. To the degree that targets can be convinced their environment is not as dangerous as they think it is, violence and damaging emotional reactions as well—could be reduced. Unfortunately, only a few members of a group need to be physical victims in order for the entire group to feel themselves vulnerable. Prisons need to be much safer than they are before men cease to predict dire consequences from slightly objective cues.

Nowadays, good correctional administrators generally protect most men from sexual assault. In its less flagrant forms, of course, sexual aggression can thrive in the most well run modern institutions, for much of it falls outside the purview of custody concerns. Sexual aggression, as we define the term, includes a wide continuum of approaches perceived to be threatening. The rate for such behavior seems likely to remain constant, regardless of improvements in security, unless there is a change in the human or social ecology of the prison community. Rates of sexual assault, on the other hand, such as those reported in the Philadelphia study, probably fluctuate drastically (especially in jails) as architecture, administrative competence, and public concern vary. Staff cannot stop the problem, but it can take measures to control it.

One control measure, which seems of limited value, consists of bringing police and courts into the picture. In our study only one incident resulted in aggressors being referred to court, and a year after the assault neither one of the two aggressors in the incident had been tried. The Philadelphia report notes a similar picture: Out of an estimated 2000 assaults, only 26 were turned over to the police for prosecution (Davis, 1968a,b). In prison, victims fear testifying, inmate observers will not come forward as witnesses, and staff can observe little illegal sexual behavior. Even if staff are eager to obtain convictions, victims fear becoming "rats" during the remainder of their sentences and are justifiably reluctant to face the humiliation and embarrassment that comes when one openly reveals one's "loss of manhood." Consequently, victims seldom urge the pressing of charges, especially when such a solution increases the chances of further victimization.

Even when cases of sexual assault are prosecuted in the courts, evidentiary standards make conviction difficult. Delays make the extended isolation of participants (victims, inmate witnesses, and aggressors) a necessity. The one case in our study where aggressors were indicted caused endless trouble for administrators, witnesses, the victim, and the aggressor–defendants. Correctional law prevented the aggressors from being sent to the "box" (disciplinary segregation) for more than 60 days. Witnesses and the victim had to be separated from aggressors and protected from harm. Forced transfers and forced isolation were the only solutions. It is not surprising that victims often give up their intentions to press charges and that the courage of some inmate witnesses fades.

Moreover, prosecution of aggressors, even if successful, can do little to improve the general situation described in this book. Much aggressor behavior is not provably illegal. While some threats and attacks may constitute bonafide violation of criminal codes, anything less than sexual assault is not likely to receive much attention in the courts. Threats and fights are the daily fare of prison; they are tolerated, viewed as normative behavior, and thought of as nothing to get upset about. Few prisoners or prison staff would be willing to define threats and minor scuffles as law violations, although they may be seen as breaches of prison discipline regulations. Attaching legal blame may also be difficult in many of the incidents we describe. Motives and intentions, as we have seen, tend to be entangled in a complex interaction.

Nor should increasing the number of guards in the prison have an appreciable effect once sexual assault is controlled. Prisoner society, as a culture existing separate from official influence, has a far greater effect on men doing time than does the formal organization of a prison. Also, the impacts we have been discussing are linked to how men view their world rather than to factual descriptions of that world. Proof of this fact comes from our interviews with men in the youth prison. The most severe target reactions—and the highest rate of target incidents—occur among youth prison inmates, the inhabitants of a bastion of rigid custodial perfection: The architectural design of the prison calls for inmates being under surveillance of staff most of the time whenever out of their single cells. Guards march men through the halls by "companies." There are enough officers, and they are well trained, and work under excellent supervision. Nonetheless, sexual victimization prevails.

Of course, in the prisons where our incidents took place, men could be locked up more carefully. Free movement could be restricted even more than it is. Ultimately, all prisoners could be isolated from contact with one another. But we suspect that, even were such draconian measures to be taken, aggressors would somehow get their message across to targets. Increasing custody reaches a point of obvious diminishing returns.

Some argue that architectural alterations will reduce the problem of victimization. Single cells are frequently mentioned as a solution. Yet most of our incidents took place in a system that gives every man a secure single cell. In prison systems lacking them, the single cell can be recommended as an improvement. But the problem still can be expected to persist, although at a lower incidence rate.

Some blame the largeness of penitentiaries for the victimization problem, claiming that smaller institutions are safer. Yet, at least in the study by Bartollas et al. (1976), sexual victimization thrived in supposedly humane "cottage" settings. We may also recall that there are substantial capital investments in large penitentiaries. Regardless of criticism, they are here to stay.

In contrast to the arguments for altering architecture or increasing custody, some writers see a solution in decreasing the control staff now have over men. Gagnon and Simon (1973), thus suggest the possibility that:

> By increasing coercion one increases the pressure to divide inmates from one another, and one decreases their capacity for self-expression and self-control. As the pressure builds, there may well be a tendency for homosexual relationships to increase in importance to the inmate population as a reaction to the intensity of the pressure. (p. 259)

Paradoxically, this implies that increasing targets' protection through custody measures may cause aggressors to have a greater need to express themselves through exploitative activity. Certainly, however, aggressors cannot be given free rein on the basis of this problematical theory. Even if there is a chance that reducing traditional security might reduce victimization, prisons have an obligation to protect men that precludes experiments with potential for allowing men to be harmed.

Another possible solution lies in "classification," the correctional process that places prisoners into appropriate groups for security and rehabilitation. Theoretically, potential targets could be placed in the least threatening jobs and cell blocks. They could be separated from those likely to be aggressors. Courts and penologists recognize this principle, and nowadays a common recommendation (or a court ordered measure) to relieve sexual aggression is "proper classification."

However, if a classification scheme were based on the statistical portrait of the man likely to be a target, virtually all young white inmates would have to be considered vulnerable. To physically separate such targets from potential aggressors would call for segregating prisons on a racial basis. Considering the equally pressing concern for integration, such a move is not an option that is generally available to administrators of public institutions. Advocates of prison integration, however, should recognize that there is some suggestion that the current situation (integration) may actually result in an increase in interracial tension and negative attitudes.

Resistance to ethnic classification could also come from white inmates themselves. Forcing men to live in certain prisons or certain areas within a prison may violate plans men make for themselves. Prisoners, for sound personal reasons, often resist what staff believe is good for them. Many prisoners may prefer coping with sexual aggression to the likelihood of being the objects of an intervention shuttling them to places they dislike. Such men might particularly resent the assumption that they cannot (or have not) handled life problems successfully themselves. Moreover, inmates may be reluctant to sacrifice benefits on the strength of a statistical prediction of danger.

Another issue is special classification, for which only the most vulnerable, the most traumatized, or those who request separation on the basis of fear could be considered (Toch, 1977). This practice does occur formally in Coxsackie and informally in other prisons. The strategy seems to work well, although it often serves men who have already had rough experiences. The biggest problem we face if we expand such procedures is the stigma issue. Men living in special settings for the weak are labeled "weak." This label can follow men for a long time and effectively reduce the help given by special classification, even making future victimization more probable.

For years, in New York State and elsewhere, "Sissy Companies" provided safe havens for homosexuals, targets, and potential targets. While offering physical protection, these separate cell blocks also restricted men to certain areas and denied them privileges enjoyed by the main population. Successful legal attacks were launched, based on the constitutional guarantee to equal protection. Consequently, there has been a move away from "Sissy Companies." They have been abolished in New York's prisons. Federal standards now discourage their use in protecting the physically attractive (Scacco, 1975). Any plan that groups targets or potential targets runs the risk of creating new "Sissy Companies" under different banners.

For years, classification has worked under the premise that separating the young from the old helps to protect younger men from exploitation. Our data suggest that sexual aggression is concentrated in youth facilities, which implies that classification on age alone not only fails to solve the problem but may increase it. Youth prisons can give more peer support and more peer temptation to exploitation. Possible restraining influences from older men are absent. As Daniel Glaser (1969) notes, youths might feel less pressure in a mixed-age institution than in an all-youth facility.

Based on the as yet unproven theory that sexual aggression stems from lack of conventional symbols of masculinity, it has been suggested that increasing and improving athletic, vocational, and educational programs will reduce drives for sexual aggression. It is argued that better programs will give potential aggressors healthier outlets than sexual aggression for masculine expression. Gagnon and Simon (1968), the forerunners of this idea, write that improved prison programming will give "alternative modes of self-expression for those social and psychological needs which, because of the current structure of the male prison, result in homosexuality" (p. 27). Davis (1968a,b) mirrors this notion in attributing the events he describes in the Philadelphia report to two main causes: (1) inadequate guard supervision, and (2) inadequate programming. Along with recommending more guards, Davis recommends athletic, vocational, and educational programs.

Our earlier discussion of aggressors, however, casts doubt on the theory that prison conditions themselves motivate sexual aggression. That chapter shows continuity between behavior on the street and behavior in the prison. Aggressors appear to be members of a "subculture of violence," and are shaped more by community subcultural forces than by any forces inherent in prison. Compulsive masculinity may indeed be part of the picture, but, if so, it is formed well before coming to prison and is probably caused more by family structure than by prison life.

Irrespective of aggressors' origins, altering such dispositions would be a difficult task. Programs aimed at changing normatively supported conduct must struggle against such factors as susceptibility to group intoxication and the resistance posed by coherent group value systems. Moreover, although our research shows that some aggressors become known to authorities after incidents, most remain unknown. This limits the value of treatment focusing on specific individuals. Predicting aggressors from background data, moreover, according to our findings, is difficult because aggressors share the characteristics of other violent offenders to a remarkable extent.

ALTERNATIVE SEXUAL OUTLETS

Another approach is providing more acceptable sexual outlets for prisoners. Although commentators discount sexual motive, aggressors tell us they are bothered by sexual deprivation and seek contact for sexual stimulation. Yet conjugal visits would not help most aggressors: At least in our study, very few aggressors are legally married or have common-law wives. Many aggressors are too young to have wives, and others are so violent and so prone to get into trouble that they lack enough "street time" to form relationships.

Aggressors also seem to be left out of home furlough programs because they fail to meet the standards for temporary release. Officials are reluctant to send such prisoners on home visits because of poor behavior. As we have seen, they tend to accumulate inordinate numbers of disciplinary infractions of all types. Thus, if furlough is a reward, aggressors become excluded. An even more important consideration limiting aggressors' legitimate sexual access is the issue of danger. While no one can predict with certainty who will commit a violent crime, we can look at some likely indicators. Aggressors, unfortunately, possess two characteristics that could lead one to predict that at least a percentage of them will be dangerous in the free world: (1) they have been openly violent while serving time, as indicated by their records for violent disciplinary infractions; and (2) they have previous records for violent criminal behavior. Therefore, aggressors, in general, are poor risks to impose upon the community.

There are sharp similarities between prison sexual aggressors and many violent youthful criminals on the street. A lower-class male subculture, including some whites but mostly made up of blacks, brings fear to prisons just as it does to New York City's darkened streets. In the free world, young men from this group, taking advantage of opportunities around them, mainly employ their violence to rob others. Because prison limits criminal opportunity but not aggressive forces, some violent offenders, while serving time, employ their violence to exploit weaker prisoners sexually. Until such time as the streets of New York City are safe, sexual aggressors will continue to operate in New York's prisons.

Sexual violence in prison, part of the general problem of youthful violence, ultimately has its roots in the economic and racial situation of our society. Unfortunately, prospects for societal improvement appear dim at this time. Moreover, individual change is also unlikely. My research indicates the contribution of subcultural values and group process to youthful violence. Obstacles to changing men motivated by such forces are formidable. Nearly all evaluations of correctional treatment have shown the money spent on changing youthful violent offenders to be wasted (Fishman, 1977; Martinson et al. 1976). In spite of pouring funds and trained staff into the effort, planned correctional change too often fails to compete with the forces violent youths acquire in their upbringing.

Incapacitation, or locking offenders up for as long as they are deemed dangerous, remains as a response to youthful crime on the streets. But what about violent sexual exploitation in prisons? What response remains if we admit the failure of correctional treatment to alter careers, such as those described in this book, significantly? Prisons that contain youthful members of the subculture of violence will remain places of fear and exploitation as long as our society continues to produce violence. Prison guards can reduce open physical assault; however, unless aggressors in prison are changed (an unlikely event given today's knowledge of correctional treatment), sexual agressors will keep their drives intact and will exert them in subtle ways that security forces are powerless to stop. Moreover, the prison of the future will probably be even more sexually aggressive than the prison of today: As the public demands more certain and more severe punishment for violent urban youths, prisons will hold higher percentages of violent offenders and, therefore, higher percentages of potential sexual aggressors.

Whom should we blame for the existence of sexual aggressors in our prisons? Some writers (Weiss and Friar, 1975; Carroll, 1977) claim the situation is almost entirely the fault of negligent or willfully evil prison staff. Indeed, improving or more closely supervising staff can reduce some aggression. However, other than effecting a return to solitary confinement for everyone, an alternative which would cause more misery than it would correct, prison staff are limited in what they can do. Prison society has always been primarily a creation of the prisoners themselves. The influence of staff on the daily lives on inmates is secondary to the influence of inmate subculture on men in confinement. Prison administrators, therefore, cannot be entirely blamed for sexual aggression.

If we cannot blame prison staff for all of the sexual aggression in prison, then can we blame American society for fostering social conditions that breed aggressive youths? Should we change our society and eliminate the subcultures producing violent youths? Wolfgang and Ferricuti (1967) suggest such a solution.

> Should the lower classes become more like the middle class in value orientation, family structure, and stability, there is reason to believe the emphasis on masculine identification through physical prowess and aggression would decline. . . . And as the disparity in life style, values, and norms between the lower and middle classes is diminished, so too will be reduced the subculture of violence that views ready resort to violence as an expected form of masculine response to many situations. . . .
>
> When the families from the subculture of violence had been distributed and increasingly absorbed by the surrounding middle-class milieu, they would become conditioned to the behavioral expectations around them. (pp. 306–307)

Eliminating the violent subculture of severe poverty, dispersing its members throughout white middle-class communities, may ultimately be the only solution that would really eliminate prison sexual aggressors. But we must balance the benefits against the costs. Dangerous precedents would be set for destroying minority values in the name of beneficent social engineering. We risk losing the richness of such culture along with its negative aspects. Because of the value we place on ethnic diversity, because of our belief in the integrity of minority life-styles, sexual aggression in prison may continue as long as prison does. It may be one cost we must pay for preventing cultural genocide.

HOPE FOR MANAGING PRISON CONFLICTS

One innovation appears to have some hope as a tool for altering this pattern of prison sexual violence: It is the Alternatives to Violence Project (AVP). Since 1975, AVP has trained over 400 New York State prison residents in nonviolence. Several of these individuals have gone on to become outstanding trainers themselves. While AVP has yet to be formally evaluated, those who have gone through its training give it good reviews. As one prisoner states, "We really did it at the last workshop. I learned a lot of things that I really didn't know about myself, and a lot of things have happened since you people [the trainers] left, and it feels good. . . . I have passed violence now . . . I feel different" (AVP, 1978, p. 1).

While AVP trainers teach conflict resolution, they also aim to alter the basic attitudes that cause offenders to get into trouble, whether in prison or in the street. Consequently, this program has the potential to reshape incidents of sexual aggression and alter the values of the aggressors initiating them. As previous chapters indicate, prison sexual violence derives as much from escalating encounters as it does from premeditated explotation. AVP's method of training prepares individuals to deescalate potentially serious conflicts through a variety of creative methods. Since prison sexual violence closely resembles other destructive encounters, a suitable response to the situation in our institutions should have as its outcome the reduction of recidivism as well as the reduction of fear, anxiety, and crisis in prison. As Lee Stern (1978) states, "Inmates take this training as much to how to deal creatively with situations they will encounter when they get out, as they do to learn how to deal constructively with the tensions and oppression inside" (p. 9).

Alternatives to Violence, the program for prison residents, resembles other organized efforts to reduce conflict in schools, demonstrations, and other settings. Part of the Quaker Project on Community Conflict (QPCC), which has its headquarters on 15 Rutherford Place in New York City, the intellectual antecedents of AVP range from the spiritual ideas of the Quaker founder, George Fox, to the more modern message of Mahatma Ghandi. QPCC has effectively combined belief in nonviolence as a way of life with modern psychological techniques for changing people and situations. This combination of spirituality and human relations training, administered by vigorous and businesslike volunteers, has proven to be a potent force in managing conflict.

AVP trainers in prison use techniques that have been thoroughly tested in such diverse settings as rock concerts, classrooms, and peace demonstrations. In Buffalo, in 1968, QPCC first began working with the criminal justice system when the Quaker group operated a project aimed at reducing conflict between minority members and the police. Thus, the Alternatives to Violence Project, now running in prisons throughout New York, is based on a substantial body of knowledge thoroughly tested in action settings.

The basic themes of AVP are the following (Stern, 1978, p. 7).

Communication: to improve listening, speaking, and observation skills.

Cooperation and Community Building: to develop a trusting, supportive atmosphere.

Affirmation: to help people feel good about themselves and others.

Conflict Resolution and Problem Solving: to explore the many creative solutions that are possible in a variety of situations.

The themes of AVP are carried out through a series of carefully structured exercises. First, these exercises cause the prisoners in the session to develop trust in one another. Then, they move on to activites such as role-playing, where inmates simulate potentially violent situations and practice dealing with them nonviolently. Trainers, all volunteers, learn to run these activities in several weekend sessions. Then they work in prisons as apprentice trainers with more experienced AVP leaders. Almost anyone who is committed to nonviolence can become a trainer. No special education is required and no professional certificate is necessary. Without a single paid staff member and without reliance on expensive professionals, AVP has worked out a method for transferring complex group process techniques to prisoners who can use them in their daily lives. Part of the success of the method lies in the fact that everyone is a volunteer, for not only are such trainers zealous, but prisoners trust them. Inmates know trainers are working with them because the trainers believe in what they are doing.

The principles of the Alternatives to Violence Program relate to the facts in the previous chapters. We have seen, for example, how prison sexual violence can result from incidents, initiated by verbal propositions that escalate into violent encounters. Targets often believe they must be violent against aggressors so that these men will leave them alone. AVP works to develop assertive but peaceful methods for accomplishing such goals. As Lawrence Apsey, the administrator of AVP, states, "The kind of nonviolence that we're talking about is being very firm and sometimes very aggressive in a nonviolent way" (Stone, 1977). Will this approach work in prison, one of the most hostile environments in which Americans live? Let us consider the obstacles that a plan such as AVP faces.

Probably one of the biggest obstacles for AVP is that the prisoners being trained must be volunteers. Thus, only those who accept the need to alter their methods of dealing with violence enter the program. Prisoners, to benefit from AVP, must be motivated to change. As we have seen, aggressors generally enter prison with histories of violence. In some cases, these men wish to become less violent so as to avoid prison in the future. They may also feel guilty about their crimes. For such persons, AVP offers hope. However, an individual with a patterned history of violent behavior often acts in such a way because he has learned that violence is proper. Violent people, unfortunately, often believe in violence. Human relations training without sincerely motivated participants can do little to alter basic value orientations. For a program such as AVP to effect sexual aggressors, aggressors must themselves realize the desirability of change. In many instances, there are no forces to bring about the belief in nonviolence. Moreover, we must consider that aggressors, like most prisoners, have been continually schooled in the value of physical force.

As we have seen, prison sexual violence ultimately is caused by violent values. These values are learned in communities, families, and peer groups. Situations in which offenders become involved reinforce these values. Economic conditions—especially high minority youth employment rates—increase incentives for robbery. Violence itself, as it leads to victimization and fear in high crime areas, causes more violence as individuals act to protect themselves through violence. Not the least influential of the situations in which one learns the value of force is involvement in the criminal justice system. While punishment for crime may be justly deserved, programs such as AVP, which call for individuals to repudiate the use of violence to solve life problems, must struggle against the contradictory examples set by the police, the courts, and the prison system. Can we ask a person to give up his or her belief in the propriety of violence when we rely on threats of punishment and physical force and constraint to manage that individual?

Similarly, the risk of abandoning a technique that "works" must be weighed against the acceptance of new methods for solving peacefully what has been heretofore solved with violence. Prison violence may be destructive. It may harm others. It may get prisoners into more trouble with the law than they are already in. However, deplorable as it may be, violence helps targets of aggressors survive. When we ask prisoners to handle situations nonviolently, we ask them to face risky situations with untried weapons. An obstacle to accepting AVP, thus, lies in the proven value of violence as a method of copying with violence.

Target violence, of course, would greatly diminish if aggressors would reform. However, such change may be dependent to a large extent on general alteration of our values. Sexual violence in prison, the work of a subculture, also has.its roots in aggressive values spread widely throughout the American people. Individual acts of rape emerge from a broad foundation of attitudes, beliefs, and behaviors favorable to sexual exploitation. Regardless of race or social class, American men, to some degree, view women as sex objects. The "little rapes"—stares and remarks—that are seen everywhere and accepted as normal behavior, are the base upon which the more violent sexual encounters are built. Since prison aggressors treat targets as women, their overall values about women and sex must be changed before prison behavior will be altered. The problem of prison sexual violence is closely linked to the general problem of sexual aggression in our society: As we progress towards transforming male attitudes towards females, we shall progress toward reducing prison sexual victimization.

References

Amir, M. 1971. *Patterns in Forcible Rape.* Chicago: University of Chicago Press, 1971.

Alternatives to Violence Project (AVP) 1978. *Newsletter* 2.

Bartollas, C., Miller, S. J., and Dinitz, S. 1976. *Juvenile Victimization.* New York: Sage Publ.

Blanchard, W. H. 1959. The group process in gang rape. *Journal of Social Psychology,* 49: 259–266.

Bloch H. 1955. Social pressures of confinement toward sexual deviation. *Journal of Social Therapy,* 1: 112–123.

Brownmiller, S. 1975. *Against Our Will.* New York: Simon and Schuster.

Buffum, P. C. 1972. *Homosexuality in Prisons.* Washington: U.S. Government Printing Office.

Bugliosi, V. 1974. *Helter Skelter.* New York: W. V. Norton.

Burgess, A. W., and Holmstrom, L. 1974. *Rape: Victims of Crisis.* Robert J. Brady Co., 1974.

Carlton, L. 1971. The terrifying homosexual world of the jail system. *The New York Times,* 25 April: 40.

Carroll, L. 1977. Humanitarian reform and biracial sexual assault in a maximum security prison. *Urban Life* 5: 417–437.

Clemmer, D. 1958. *The Prison Community.* Boston: Christopher Publ. House.

Cohen, A. K., Cole, G. F., and Bailey, R. G. 1976. *Prison Violence.* Lexington, Mass.: Lexington Books.

Cohen, M. L. 1971. The psychology of rapists. *Seminars in Psychiatry.* 303: 312–325.

Conrad, J. P. 1966. Violence in prison. *Annals of the American Academy of Political and Social Sciences* 364: 113–119.

Davis, A. J. 1968a. Report on sexual assaults in the Philadelphia prison system and sheriff's vans. Philadelphia District Attorney's Office and the Police Department. Unpublished manuscript.

Davis, A. J. 1968b. Sexual assaults in the Philadelphia prison system and sheriff's vans. *Trans-Action.* 6: 8–16.

Davis, A., and Dollard, J. 1964. *Children of Bondage.* New York: Harper.

Ehrmann, W. 1964. Marital and nonmarital sexual behavior. In *Handbook of Marriage and the Family.* Christensen, H. T., ed. Chicago: Rand McNally, pp. 585–622.

Finestone, H. 1957. Cats, kicks, and color. *Social Problems* 5: 3–13.

Fishman, R. 1977. An evaluation of criminal recidivism in projects providing rehabilitation and diversion services in New York City. *The Journal of Criminal Law and Criminology* 68: 283–305.

Fox, J. G. 1976. Self imposed stigmata: A study of tattooing among female inmates. Doctoral dissertation, State University of New York at Albany. Ann Arbor, Mich.: Xerox University Microfilms.

Fuller, D. A., Orsagh, T., and Raber, D. 1976. Violence and victimization within the North Carolina prison system. Unpublished manuscript.

Gagnon, J. H., and Simon, W. 1968. The social meaning of prison homosexuality. *Federal Probation* 32: 23–29.

Gagnon, J. H., and Simon, W. 1973. *Sexual Conduct.* Chicago: Aldine.

Gardner, M. R. 1975. The defense of necessity and the right to escape from prison—a step towards incarceration free from sexual assault. *Southern California Law Review* 49: 110–152.

Geis, G. 1971. Group sexual assaults. *Medical Aspects of Human Sexuality,* May: 101–112.

Giallombardo, R. 1966. *Society of Women.* New York: John Wiley and Sons.

Gibbs, J. 1978. Jailing and stress. Doctoral dissertation, State University of New York at Albany. Ann Arbor, Mich.: Xerox University Microfilms.

Glaser, D. 1969. *The Effectiveness of a Prison and Parole System.* New York: Bobbs-Merrill.

Goffman, I. 1961. *Asylums.* New York: Doubleday.

Gold, M. 1970. *Delinquent Behavior in an American City.* Belmont, Calif.: Brooks/Cole.

Gold, M. 1958. Suicide, homicide and the socialization of aggression. *American Journal of Sociology* 63: 651–661.

Hofstadter, R., and Wallace, M. (eds.) 1970. *American Violence.* New York: Vintage.

Holsti, O. R. 1969. *Content Analysis for the Social Sciences and Humanities.* Reading, Mass.: Addison-Wesley.

Holt vs Sarver 1971. 442 F. 2d, 304.

Huffman, A. 1960. Sex deviation in a prison community. *Journal of Social Therapy* 6: 170–181.

Irwin, J. 1971. Some research questions on homosexuality in jails and prisons. Unpublished paper.

Johnson, R. 1976. *Culture and Crisis in Conflict.* Lexington, Mass.: Lexington Books.

Kanin, E. J., and Kirkpatrick, D. 1953. Male sex aggression on a university campus. *American Sociological Review* 22: 52–58.

Kanin, E. J. 1957. Male aggression in dating–courtship relations. *American Journal of Sociology* 63: 197–204.

Kanin, E. J. 1965. Male aggression and three psychiatric hypotheses. *Journal of Sex Research* 1: 221–231.

Kanin, E. J. 1967. An examination of sexual aggression as a result of sexual frustration. *Journal of Marriage and Family* 29: 428–433.

Karpman, B. 1948. Sex life in prison. *Journal of Criminal Law and Criminology* 3: 475–486.

King, W. 1975. Rise in inmates strains jails of south: Florida jams 10 into 12-by-15 foot cells. *The New York Times,* 24 October: A-1, C-10.

Lockwood, D. 1977a. Living in protection. In *Survival in prison.* Toch, H., ed. New York: The Free Press.

Lockwood, D. 1977b. Sexual aggression among male prisoners. Ph.D. Dissertation, State University of New York at Albany.

Lockwood, D. 1978. Maintaining manhood: Prison violence precipitated by aggressive sexual overtures. Paper prepared for the Academy of Criminal Justice Sciences, March.

Martin, R., et al. 1974. The account of the white house seven. *Friends Journal* (1 October): 484–499.

Martinson, R., Palmer, T., and Adams, S. Rehabilitation, recidivism, and research. Hackensack, N.J.: National Council on Crime and Delinquency.

Miller, D., and Levy, M. 1970. *Going to Jail.* New York: Grove Press.

Nettler, Q. 1977. *Explaining Crime.* New York: McGraw-Hill.

New York State Special Commission on Attica 1974. *Attica.* New York: Praeger.

New York Times 1974a. Panel says an informed public would demand prison reform. 7 March: C-18. Report of House Judiciary subcommittee headed by Representative Robert W. Kastenmeir (D. Wis.).

New York Times 1974b. Killing of Carolina jailer, charged to woman, raises question of abuse of inmates. 1 December.

New York Times 1975a. Four advertisers drop spots on repeat of "Born Innocent." 25 October: M-47.

New York Times 1975b. Ex-inmate tells of sexual abuse. 19 November: F-20.

Patterson, H., and Conrad, E. 1950. *Scottsboro Boy.* New York: Doubleday.

Radzinowicz, L. 1957. *Sexual Offenses.* London: Macmillan.

Redl, F. 1949. The phenomenon of group contagion and shock effect in group therapy. In *Searchlight on Delinquency.* Eissler, K. R., ed. New York: International University Press, pp. 315–328.

Roth, L. H. 1971. Territoriality and homosexuality in a male prison population. *American Journal of Orthopsychiatry* 41: 510–513.

Scacco, A. M. 1975. *Rape in Prison.* Springfield, Ill.: Thomas.

Schafer, S. 1977. *Victimology: The Victim and His Criminal.* Reston, Va.: Reston Publ. Co.

Schultz, L. G. 1964. The victim–offender relationship. *Crime and Delinquency* 14: 135–141.

Shaw, C. R. 1966 *The Jack-Roller.* Chicago: The University of Chicago Press.

Slim, I. 1967. *Pimp: The Story of My Life.* Holloway House. Quoted in Armstrong, G. 1971. *Life at the Bottom.* New York: Bantam, pp. 232–237.

Srivastava, S. P. 1974. Sex life in an Indian male prison. *Indian Journal of Social Work* 3: 21–33.

Stern, Lee. 1978. Creative response to conflict and violence. *Fellowship Magazine,* November: 7–9.

Stone, Marilyn. 1977. A different approach to solving the world's violence. *Poughkeepsie Journal,* 26 December.

Sykes, G. M. 1971. *The Society of Captives.* Princeton: Princeton University Press.

Task Force for Institutional Violence 1965. Aggressive history profile and known reason for violence against victims (CDC and YA combined). Unpublished manuscript, California Department of Corrections.

Teresa, V. 1973. *My Life in the Mafia.* Greenwich, Conn.: Fawcett.

Thomas, P. 1967. *Down These Mean Streets.* New York: New American Library.

Times Union (Albany) 1975a. Escapee tells of prison attacks. 22 April: 4.

Times Union (Albany) 1975b. 6 indicted in sodomy at Dutchess Co. jail. 31 May: 6.

Toby, J. 1966. Violence and the masculine ideal: Some qualitative data. In *Patterns of Violence.* Wolfgang, M. E., ed. *The Annals of the American Academy of Political and Social Science* 64: 19–27.

Toch, H. 1975. Institutional violence code, tentative code of the classification of inmate assaults on other inmates. Unpublished manuscript, California Department of Corrections Research Division.

Toch, H. 1969. *Violent Men.* Chicago: Aldine.

Toch, H. 1975. *Men in Crisis: Human Breakdowns in Prison.* Chicago: Aldine.

Toch, H. 1977. *Living in Prison.* New York: The Free Press.

U.S. Department of Justice 1977. *Criminal Victimization in the United States.* National crime survey report SD-NCS-N-8. Washington, D.C.: U.S. Government Printing Office.

U.S. Department of Justice 1960. Uniform Crime Reports. Washington, D.C.

Ward, J. L. 1958. Homosexual behavior of the institutionalized delinquent. *Psychiatric Quarterly Supplement* 32: 301–314.

Weiss, C., and Friar, D. J. 1975. *Terror in the Prisons.* New York: Bobbs-Merrill.

Wolfgang, M. E., and Ferracuti, F. 1967. *The Subculture of Violence.* London: Tavistock

Index